SHERMANDA ANDERSON RAMSAY

FORWARDS BY:

Dr. Lori

America's #1 Fat Loss Expert, Health Expert for ABC TV Show 'Good Morning Texas', Best-Selling and Author of 'Fire-Up Your Fat Burn!' at DLS HealthWorks

Dr. Bob Choats

"Transformational Grandmaster", America"s #1 Mind-Body Transformation Expert and author

Mind Your Own Fitness', Trainer & Professional Speaker at Optimal Life Seminars

Sofie Nubani

Co-Founder of Laughter Mindset, a Visionary on a Mission helping people Reach their Full Potential

A Winning World

First Edition

Copyright © 2018 by Shermanda Ramsay

Cover and internal design © Shermanda Ramsay

Published by Shermanda Ramsay- Write Road Publishing

ALL RIGHTS RESERVED. No part of this book can be reproduced in any form or by any electronic or mechanical

Means, including information storage, retrieval systems, photocopying, recording or otherwise – except in the case of brief quotations embodied in articles or reviews giving proper creation credit to the publisher Shermanda Ramsay - without permission in writing from its publisher, Shermanda Ramsay, A Winning World, Corp.

All brand names and product names used in this book are trademarks, registered trademarks or trade names of their respective holders.

To my God who I attribute my ability to have the strength and fortitude to continue striving to overcome life's trials and circumstances. For HIM Loving me when I can't, haven't and/or didn't know how to love myself. For teaching me and never leaving me even when I fall, he picks me up and is always there. I truly believe that without God I could do nothing and with HIM I can do all things. When My Love Fails ME, HIS LOVE NEVER FAILS!

Forewords for A Winning World

Lori L. Shemek, PhD, CNC

We live in a world full of amazing human beings. The author of this book is one of them. I met Shermanda through mutual friends and how lucky for me! She is an amazing woman doing so much good in the world and when she asked me to write the foreword for her beautiful book Winning World, I was truly honored. I immediately began to think of the seen and unseen, the myriad of people who have stepped into challenges or fears before me or even the challenges they face presently, as I write this foreword.

Shermanda has been given a task to fulfill and why she recognized the need to create an anthology or collection of those people who not only have a story to tell but have taken that journey. Really think about this, every single author in her book has had a challenge that most of us have likely not encountered and this is the key. These individuals are disseminating their distilled lessons without us having to literally go through the experience. Shermanda's story is one of those patriots, making her, and the collection of other authors, a true gift to this world. She has been through what most feel they could not go through, and yet despite her intentions, life had something else planned and she is triumphant in the end and

so can you be!

None of us are immune to what life can dish out and that would also include me. We all have challenges in life – some small and some so large we don't know which way to turn. There are those whose life has been ripped apart quickly and yet, others experience the slow and deliberate challenges. Yet, if we are open to it, we will feel a vital part of this winning world and its wisdom.

We all have a story. When I was younger, I would have said I would like a story with as few obstacles as possible. However, now I appreciate them in how they have enriched me and ultimately to those who are a part of my life experience. My early life was a series of challenges that taught me very early on the gift of life, love and lessons. I was raised by a single mother who had a constant stream of different health conditions. She tried her best to raise us; three children of whom I was the oldest and she did this alone. She had no husband, no family, no money and so because of these contributing factors; she suffered not only poor health, but chronic stress as well. I remember, often, walking into her room and seeing her laying there, in the dark suffering. However, even at my young age, I knew intuitively my mother could make different choices; she smoked over a pack of cigarettes a day, she was very overweight, she had a terrible diet, poor health and you can imagine all these factors combined with her chronic stress would not make for a healthy or quality life. As time went on, my mother's health dwindled and sadly, she passed away at the very young age of 36 years old, leaving behind three young children with nowhere to go. My two younger brothers and I would never live together again as we went to different homes. The reason I emphasize these points in my story is because we all

have choices to make in life. Every day we are given thousands of opportunities to make choices and they can either help us or hinder us.

Another aspect to living life your way, is to expect and face the power of challenges that will most assuredly come our way. Great human beings never have it easy. Look at anyone in history and you will find that with greatness, in whatever form it is cloaked in, that greatness was rife with challenges.

So how does one overcome adversity and rise above?

The way in which you perceive adversity will either allow you break free from its chains of heartache, depression, confusion, guilt, and fear or allow you to be enmeshed negatively for a lifetime that will leave its mark in every aspect of your life.

Writing this foreword is truly an honor, but what is more of an honor is my connection with you the reader, the co-creation with Shermanda and her collection of gifted, beautiful souls she has gathered together in this book to help make our world better ~ a winning world.

With Love,

BOB CHOAT

Years ago, I first started reading the Chicken Soup for the Soul book

series by Mark Victor Hansen and Jack Canfield. Within each book I found wonderful stories. The stories were by different authors. Many of whom were able to have an impact.

One such story from the first Chicken Soup for the Soul book that I remember was about 6-year old Frank "Bopsy" Salazar who had leukemia. If you haven't read it, you can find it online. To this day, that story has stuck with me and has been told many times by many speakers. I continue to search for powerful stories and always will.

You see, stories can have an inspired impact. Stories can move us to action. Stories grab us from our soul. Stories help to create nations, religions, businesses, inspire people to help the less fortunate, win wars, create a movement, and even send a man to the moon. Stories can even work against us when filled with a negative imagination.

We are guided by stories, not facts. Personal stories of people overcoming challenges and built with a lesson do certainly inspire.

Each story in Shermanda's book, A Winning World, may serve to inspire you. Each one takes place from each author's personal history of overcoming some struggle or challenge. When you read them, I'm sure you'll learn and be inspired. I'm inspire by the project itself and I will share many of these amazing stories in my talks. You may be touched by one, a few, or all the stories. When you feel a tug in your heart and feel inspired, use what you learned from each story, and take action on what you learned. Allow the stories that resonate with you to serve as a catalyst for your personal mission.

You will learn of the journey that Sofie Nubani took coming from the Middle East to the United States and defying tradition to make her own imprint as a woman and wise soul. There's Manny Garcia's journey as a child (kidnapped by his own father) and overcoming his childhood struggles to transform into the leader he has become today. You will certainly get a lot from each story contained in this book. There are many more and including mine. Shermanda's own story, is one such story of overcoming challenges. As she struggled to overcome the injuries from being hit by a vehicle, she learned to become a winner, using her challenges to help propel her to new heights. While bedridden, she's authored several books and is making an impact. A Winning World is her latest book venture that she has engaged in. Her focus on helping others has led her to have her own radio show. I am very happy to contribute my personal story to this book and to call Shermanda my friend.

I wish each and every one of you a powerful journey through life. May you one day inspire others with the story of your personal challenges as you become a winner in life as the winners you will read about here in the A Winning World anthology.

Sofie Nubani

Throughout history the power of story has been able to create nations, make changes, and have impact. There is a great power in storytelling. Those of influence should have a sense of responsibility to speak up, share and pass forward of how they were able to overcome their unfavorable circumstances.

When I connected with Shermanda Ramsay it was an instant connection of a surge field of love and light frequencies charging our field. Listening to her personal story and the inspiration of writing this book was so touching to my soul. Here is a lady who was hit by a vehicle while preparing to go provide her tutoring business afterschool services at a local school. Instead of being concerned about herself, Shermanda started talking to the lady who struck her with her vehicle. That lady was hysterical, apologizing she didn't see her and "Sweet" Shermanda consoled her.

When I asked Shermanda what was her first reaction after dealing with her progressing pain (that led her to need a cane and then a walker and later she was in a wheelchair), she said she told herself,

"I will get over it, It won't be long before I'm back on my feet, busy, running as before, with a smile." During Shermanda's bedrest in the past three years she has written six books and published three and A Winning World would be her fourth published book. She also has begun ghostwriting; taking a transcription and helping others author their own books to share their stories. Being an entrepreneur and speaker and involved in ministry Shermanda's mindset is triumphant, even while she is in bed recovering. She might have been limited in her physical movement, but not limited in her vision or mindset. From the age of 6 she asked her mother, "Why is there always Bad News on TV, why we don't see Good News." When she was giving an opportunity to host her own show for a radio station, and she began the A Winning World radio show, her vision as a child came back and she was reminded of her childhood desire to see and hear the good news being broadcast. When she started this process, this anthology was originally meant as a woman's book, but she was shown in a dream to look at the body as whole; family and spirit, men, women, and children. Her vision expanded to a global reach and her hope, faith and determination to lead, inspire and encourage those with similar challenges to have hope to dig deep and connect to their inner power was born.

Shermanda continues improving. She spends time in her wheel chair only for long distances and is using a walker daily to gain her independence again. She refuses to give up and die and decided to fully live. She shared this, "if you're still breathing, you're winning." Her faith has carried her further than most would that go through similar challenges. She is here wanting to have an impact and not just to make a difference.

I am so grateful to be part of this anthology and to be connected to some simply amazing souls. This book and stories within will inspire many who may be going through tough times as well. Learning from those who were or who are in similar circumstances (who have overcome their obstacles & struggles) is oftentimes the lift or encouragement needed to help another win. Each story presented in this book are of those who have chosen to live on purpose, Today. Each author is serving their personal mission, leading and helping others overcome their challenges. As you read each story, perhaps you will find your personal mission from your personal struggles, then share it, write about it and pass it forward. Therefore, I'm here. I saw and see Shermanda's mission and heart. I totally agree with her, support her and truly know this is a movement to bring transformation and healing to the world.

"There is no greater agony than bearing an untold story inside you."

Maya Angelou

Sending you much love and light. Blessings & Namaste.

Sofie Nubani, "The Queen of Laughter & Wisdom"

CONTENTS

Introduction Forwards

14	From Prison to Success	John "Doc" Fuller
19	Jarnell Stokes Story	Jarnell Stokes
26	Finding My Way	Printella Bankhead
33	Jehovah Jireh	Dr. E. j. Ebuk
36	The Gift of Adversity	Marcus Anderson
40	The Struggle/Journey to My Winning Life	Renato Tanamach
43	The Good the Bad and The Ugly	Laura Herndon
45	Winning Transparency in Marriage	Kristina Davidson
51	Fight to Win	Dr. BJ Fletcher
53	Surviving Against the Odds	Victoria Blackman
57	Manny Garcia Story	Manny Garcia
65	Journey To Healing	Ilonka van P-Heijster
69	Overcoming Childhood Scars	Dr. Joe Bankhead
76	Overcoming My Greatest Obstacles	Bob Choat
83	Journey To Find Purpose & Relevance	Adonia Dickson
91	Hope For Nasenyi Foundation	David Daka
94	You Can't Win Being Average	Tuan Nguyen
98	Pushed Into My Destiny	Yolando Ayo
102	Endings and Beginnings	Sofie Nubani
115	Step Into Your Greatness	Dr. Patrick Businge
118	Don't Get Held Hostage To A Job	Towanda Young
122	Dreams Trapped Behind A Desk	Keisha Adair Swaby
134	From Secret To Success	Jacqueline Moise
142	My Healing Came From The Lord	Gilbert Wanyonyi
145	Be The Change	Christopher Brauel
149	The Gift of Conviction	Shermanda Ramsay

Representing: New Jersey

John "Doc" Fuller

From Prison to Success: Transforming Your Greatest Mistake into Your Biggest Triumph

Growing up in Keyport, New Jersey, John Fuller was a self-described wayward youth. Influenced by his peers and drawn toward poor decisions, John dabbled in petty crimes. It was a hobby that was soon to become a habit. By the age of 23, John was living in Los Angeles, California, where the life of crime looked for different than the criminal life in New Jersey. In Los Angeles, high crime led to high pay checks. There was money, there was glitz, there was glamour. In Hollywood, it felt like anything was possible.

During those years, he left behind those simplistic petty crimes. Those were child's play compared to what he uncovered in the city. Soon, he was pimping and dealing drugs. He was committing forgery, creating and disseminating counterfeit money and even selling fake documentation to those who wanted to falsify their citizenship. His friends from the past see direct parallels with the character, Frank Abagnale Jr., portrayed by Leonardo DiCaprio in the hit movie Catch Me If You Can.

It was a fast-paced life. The rush of crime fueled John, leading him to commit mistake after mistake. The whirlwind stopped quickly, however, when the justice system caught up to him. Before he knew it, he was sitting in a state prison facing a one-year sentence for forgery. He did his time but went right back to his old ways. Within eight months, he was arrested again and once again found himself sitting in a prison cell.

For the following decade, his home was various cell blocks. Due to assaults against fellow inmates and other misconduct he was transferred in and out of more than 6 federal prisons as he served his sentence for conspiracy to distribute cocaine. Many people who spend a significant amount of time in prison find themselves feeling hopeless, and often for good reason. This is a dark and lonely time in anyone's life, and the criminal justice system can feel like a spiral for which there is no escape.

For Fuller, there were some desperately dark days in prison. It's not like they portray in the movies. Prisoners are witnesses to sights that people should never have to see. During his time in prison, he saw inmates being stabbed. He watched rape happen before his eyes. He saw prisoners being pimped out by other prisoners. He also participated in assaults against known pedophiles, informants and men known to commit crimes against women. It was no wonder that so many prisoners suffered from mental health disorders and emotional trauma. This was no place for the weak.

Luckily, John Fuller discovered that during his time in prison, he could still fulfill his potential, transform his life and help others — all while serving his prison sentence. He found opportunities to work directly with other inmates, particularly those who were suffering from depression and battling with suicidal thoughts. He began to mentor newcomers to the prison system, showing them how they could use their time wisely and improve themselves while serving their time. It was through this work that he was able to look past those dark moments and see the light at the end of the tunnel.

In the months immediately following his release, John knew that he didn't want to give up his work with other prisoners. He began working with criminals and teaching them about the reality of prison. He helped those who had been sentenced learn to manage and cope with daily life in prison. He began to speak to communities and at-risk populations to help reduce crime through his inspirational and motivational stories.

It didn't take long for him to discover that he had a talent. He knew that he was an effective life coach, one that could help people turn their lives around and allow them to fulfill their true goals. In every sense, John Fuller was living proof of that possibility. He was once a hardened criminal who enjoyed his life of crime — but he saw the error of his ways and transformed those poor choices into an opportunity to serve others in the community.

For some, those years in prison change everything, and not for the better. Rather than being depressed, resentful or bitter, John decided to use his time in prison to reflect on his mistakes, discover his true identity and build his self-confidence. He owned up to the fact that he had a rough start and that he didn't make the best decisions during that time. But he knew that didn't have to define his entire life. He emerged from behind those prison bars as a determined man who was ready to succeed, and he wanted to share that determination with others.

Fast forward to present day, where John Fuller is that successful man that he always knew he could be. While he's remained committed to his original purpose and passion that he discovered during his time in prison, he now has a new mission. He uses his past experiences to save people from a harrowing life of crime, he works to prepare those who are heading into their prison sentences and he actively helps inmates readjust and acclimate to society again.

To ask John Fuller to describe his occupation or his job title would be difficult. He wears so many hats, including that of a prison coach, a professional motivational speaker, a CLE trainer for criminal defense attorney, and an author who was written two books. He's proud of those accomplishments, but he's most satisfied knowing that he has helped countless people define their personal lives, create a better future for themselves and uncover their potential.

John Fuller's clients often call him an inspiration. They are impressed with the fact that he is not only willing to share his story, but that he actively works to guide those who have found themselves in similar circumstances to his own past life. He is upfront and honest, describing the events that led up to him losing his relationships with close family members and friends. He often describes his regret over the lost time and the lost freedom. He states these facts plainly, showcasing that a life of crime was not worth the consequences.

It's this unique background that makes him a leader in the criminal justice field. People listen to him because they trust him. He speaks to them in a language that they understand. He provides them with resources and facts in a way that is straightforward and honest. They believe in him because he isn't lecturing them — he is showing them that he lives out what he says. He has an inimitable style that allows him to connect easily with the people he works with, and those in the audience appreciate his entertaining, motivating and honest stories.

John Fuller has been featured on Fox News, Entertainment Tonight, CNN Headline News, Access Hollywood, Today Show Extra, North Jersey Newspapers, New York Post, and Loaded Magazine. He is available for speaking engagements at corporate events, colleges, high schools and community events. He teaches CLE Courses to criminal defense attorneys and law enforcement officials.

Those who are interested in hearing his story and learning what they can do to improve their lives, their careers or their choices each day are invited to contact him. He is ready and willing to work with anyone who could benefit from his timely and relevant message.

John with Mike Tyson and Ice T back in the day!

Representing: Tennessee

Jarnell Stokes Journey

For those of you who don't know me, I'm a professional basketball player and until recently my entire life was built around my passion of basketball and fame. Born in the heart of Memphis, I remember most of my childhood being heavily infested with anger and frustration. Where I'm from, fighting makes you the cool kid on the block. Honestly, I rode the bench my entire childhood, must've been in over 30 fights during my lifetime and couldn't articulate English as well.

At the end of the day, I think we all struggle to find the things which make us happy and complete and many times the things we think that will make us happy do not until we open up to bigger experiences.

I am a better man today because of my mindfulness through my unique experiences. This past year in Denver was a dream come true. Not only was I surrounded by young talented players and coaches I also loved the people in the front office and I vibed very well with the city.

As a matter of fact, the city of Denver oozes potential in so many ways that I've yet to see anywhere else. Yes, that includes Miami. This third year in the NBA was the best yet because the young jitters were gone and now people in the league had gotten a chance to see what I can do.

Before I had come to the Denver Nuggets, I had played in 2014 for the Miami Heat and the Memphis Grizzlies. Previously, I'd just won a G League championship, MVP and finals MVP, while leading my teammates to a historic record-breaking season. I had no idea how spoiled I was from the NBA's constant perks. Every day was a mental challenge to maintain my professionalism, even though I couldn't fathom that I'd been one foot out the league. It got to the point where I'd make it my goal to take all my anger out on every matchup opponent, especially the ones that were sent down from the NBA teams. But that's a story for another day.

My point is in order to better my life off the court and manifest new blessings, I'd have to humble myself and simplify my goals. I'd have to accept that my game needed improvement and that I'm only a G League player (until proven otherwise), but I'm going to be the best one every time I touch the floor. Who cares about the private flights, 24/7 customer service, or being famous, right? Limiting my pessimistic thoughts in every moment gave me the opportunity to work on some things I hadn't previously got the notion to do, such as, studying X's and O's, long range shooting skills, charisma in diverse crowds, and different perspectives of mental toughness. I chose to embrace the new. It wasn't easy as I learned this later that year. It paid off. The following year I was back in the NBA. So back to my time in Denver...

Loving my team and appreciating the opportunity, my year in Denver gave me a huge morale boost to work even harder. I would watch film on defending and even learned in-person from great defenders like scout, Chuck Hayes. I strived to be the first in the gym and the last to leave it. I've always been motivated and hard-working but the fact that pinnacle had been reached made me more determined than ever. Never had I been more confident in my abilities to rebound, score, defend and even expand to shooting 3's. I'd worked my ass off to destroy any obstacle that could hold me back from my destiny.

> Everybody has gone through trials and tribulations that has unexpectedly altered or shifted their path towards a desirable intention and energy. Choose wisely. -Jarnell Stokes

This third year was going to be my year and it was as if things finally came together. From years of conditioning and training, my body moved like a well-oiled machine and my mind was strong and clear. I also began working on my spiritual strength too in order to become a trifecta of determination. Mentally and physically, I was ready, and I knew this was a spot that I had earned. Every morning, I'd get up and try to tweet a few words of wisdom, attend chapel before games sparking alliances with other players and attend yoga to relax my mind. Everything about me was going to be as strong as possible, in my plan.

> *"If you don't know me or what I know, I won't expect you to understand me or see what I see." -Jarnell Stokes*

I had an amazing start to the season, while playing for the Nuggets, I got a standing ovation playing in the FedEx Forum against the Memphis Grizzlies and that meant the world to me, coming from my hometown and the team I used to play for. Not only was I happy with my pinnacle to this point, people recognized it too and that was an extremely proud moment for me. There is nothing like hard work paying off. This was it. This was my dream. It was actually happening. The life I'd been chasing, dreaming and praying for was manifesting before my eyes.

Everybody was so supportive too. I got a lot of hometown love, from my visits to St. Jude to getting recognized in the nightclubs. Imagine if you were able to play professional basketball for the team you grew up admiring as a kid. I'd visit my family members from the hood in complete shock of how much they had my back. For instance, I'd visit my grandma and aunt telling them I felt as if I could've done a better job competing for playing time, but in their eyes "Coach is hating on my baby. You're too good not to be playing. "So-and-so can't coach," they'd say. "Such-and such can't pass." Family... Gotta love 'em.

I stepped onto the court one night and it was any other game and I was ready to give it my all and give the team a boost. So, on November 2nd, I checked into the game against the Golden State Warriors. In just six minutes of play, I finished the game with 2 points, 2 assists, and a few rebounds. An article had me listed as leading the league in PER for 2 consecutive years. I remember reading it and being amused because those stats were without the minute requirements. Those type of efficient numbers right there was what I was getting paid the millions to do. Finishing the game, I was happy with my performance...but something felt wrong. Little did I know this something would change my life forever.

I could hear my heart beating. I could sense the worry from my teammates. "Stay positive" is what I'd tell myself, but my actions showed otherwise. My foot was bothering me more than it should have. In sports, there is 'hurt' and then there is 'injured' and this felt worse than just hurt. Hurt is the kind that you can walk off and injured is something that ends seasons and careers. After the game and my 6 minutes of glory, I went in to get an X-ray from the team doctor. Upon review, the doctor told me I had a fracture. I was sure that couldn't be true, my foot couldn't be fractured. I begged him over and over to do another X-Ray. After all, a fracture is extremely easy to misread in an X-ray and I prayed that he was reading it wrong. I was praying his diagnosis was wrong. I was praying that I could just walk this hurt off and go back to playing like nothing was wrong. I prayed that the X-ray came back fine the second time. Praying was the only thing I could do.

My prayers were answered, but not the way I had wanted. My answer was a confirmed fracture. This was my first injury. I had been hurt before, but I had never been injured before. Literally, I could not play. Where had my injury come from? One of the downfalls, to being a hard worker, is not getting enough rest to recover. This fracture definitely happened over time and one day that was enough, my foot literally broke under the constant pressure. For the first time, I had a physical limitation that I could not walk off, ice for the evening or rest. I wasn't ready to use crutches and I sure wasn't ready to take a break from the game. I was a new player and I was worried about my professional future. The day after the official diagnosis I got a call from Tim Connelly, GM of the Nuggets. A players worse nightmares confirmed and I'd have to leave the team.,,,,,

As I was put on physical rest, I realized that I wasn't ready for life after basketball, or life as a regular human being who didn't have to worry about practice, training or playing……. *This nightmare was actually happening*, but I understood that being world-class skills requires reinvention of self.

I felt as though this injury, though not catastrophic, was causing irreparable damage in my life and I had no idea how to handle it. This image of an athlete that I had created for myself during the course of my life had helped me create my identity and without it, what was I to do? Admittedly, I spiraled after my diagnosis and I started to have deep reflections of all my past failures, seemingly all at once, and how I could have ended up at this point and what I could have done differently.

I'd been so mentally prepared that there was no way I was going to let this break me.

I know I had been told I could be re-signed but truly, I found myself back at square one and I was devastated. I felt as though I had let myself, my team and my family down. This brought heavy reflections on my career as a player from being the worst kid on the team up until being ranked number #3 in high school to being drafted to my home team, Memphis Grizzlies.

Sitting around with my fractured foot, all the hard work, time spent in the chapel and even all the prayer felt like wasted time. Literally years of my life had been spent creating an identity for myself which included the title of athlete. It was who I was and what I mastered. Before the contracts, the perks and the lifestyle I had spent years of my life playing ball just because I loved it. The fact that there were perks involved made no difference at the end of the day because taking away the perks of basketball were not nearly as important as taking away my identity. My literal self-worth and identity were defined through this one thing. This injury made me realize that this is really about identity. This is about self-worth. This is about life. I was about to find out what I actually needed and why it was so much important than all the things I thought I had wanted.

How much does a dream cost? I kept thinking about a quote my mom always told me growing up which was, *"money comes, and money goes but wisdom evolves, and wisdom grows."* I didn't think about it very hard until I was faced with this identity crisis.

All of the talks over the years with my parents and older brother, teachers and coaches, and even strangers living in the mountains of Denver at the time, started to make sense.

I remembered my sophomore year, playing college ball in Tennessee, Nicodemus my strength coach would always tell me to be *thankful for storms in life because storms reveal commitment.* Sounds crazy, but what he said made so much sense and my life story didn't seem so bad suddenly. I could somewhat relate from losing hold of the dream.... Priorities are everything in this universe. He reminded me of a message Coach Martin, college coach lived by and that's aligning your priorities with your daily diet. I'm not talking food. It's what you do on the daily basis that shapes your future. Simple right? If you want to be a pro baller, then workout. If you want to be a park ranger, spend time in nature. If you believe that there's a God that rules, then fight to live by his commandments and you'll be happy.

Right? Let's give it a try for once, but with words and not daily actions or diet it adds up to nothing. So, my mission in Denver went from training my body to training my spirit and opening my mind to seek knowledge and understanding of the universe.

"When your source of joy comes from above NOTHING on this Earth can steal it from you."-Jarnell Stokes

My foot fracture and time away from the NBA was a real turning point for me. Weird things started to happen soon after. I had suddenly lost toxic energies, shed old skins and gained life skills for the future.

Instead of waking up to social media, I'd wake up to meditate, practice gratitude, read self help books, and thrive in the daily word. Eventually I found myself hanging with more supportive crowds and changing habits entirely. I only wanted positive, empowering things in my life and body.

Somehow, I also grew closer to good energies, such as, a few of my creative partners and mentors, Dr. Lori Shemek, Howard Flamm, Denise McDermott, that I'd normally ignore for training. To make a long story short, we later started "Stoked Fitness and Media" to transform physique and consciousness and "Creation Nation Animation", a publishing company that creates and inspires great children's books (more on that later!). STOKED that I've been accepted to co-author and create a cartoon sports hero named 'Jarnac.' I'd always dreamed of being an entrepreneur and filmmaker and never felt like the life of an athlete would solely help me achieve all of my creative aspirations, though I enjoy my job to the fullest. I am ready and embracing change to evolve. I'm creating my own destiny, with a connection with God, only experience could teach. To be honest, I've never been happier, STOKED and I'm so honored to share my journey with you.

To keep up with my story, **follow me** @**jarnellstokes**. 2 Peter 3:9

Representing: Florida

FINDING MY WAY by Printella Bankhead

In 2001, I was divorced and working two jobs to make ends meet. I remember saying to myself there has to be a better way. At that time, I believed, like so many other people, that working hard was the only way to achieve the American dream. I thought that if I wanted a decent life, I had work two jobs. Soon, I found myself saying, "There has to be a better way to make a living." I realized that I was missing a lot of fun things like hanging out with friends, going to family gatherings, and simply relaxing.

I had often thought of starting my own business, but I had no clue as to what type of business I was going to start. I did a few side jobs like tax preparation, real estate investing, and other things, but none brought me the lifestyle I wanted, nor did I feel I had found my place and purpose in life. Eventually I took a job working as a security officer because of a suggestion from someone. I worked at a church for several years part-time along with my full-time job. As I worked hard, I began to seek answers to life challenges. One day something happened that changed my life completely, my Pastor asked me if I had ever thought of starting my own business. He told me that he thought that I had what it took and that he had a lot of respect for how diligent I was with my job. He shared that he was sure if I worked like that in my own business it would be successful. I was a little reluctant and fearful of taking such a big step. A few weeks passed, and he called me to his office and asked if I had given it any thought. I told him yes, but I had not taken any action. More time passed, and finally I made the step toward having my own business. The rest is history, and I would like to share my success story. I was able to succeed at finding my true passion by taking step one, setting goals, writing and quoting affirmations, using the law of attraction, visualizing, practicing gratitude, and working with others who had also asked that same question that I had asked myself. I would like to share how powerful and effective those methods have been for me. I am so convinced and excited about how to achieve success that I would like to share this information with as many people as possible, because it changed my life. The process is very powerful. You may not get it right away, but just get started, take that first step and you will be on your way to a new life.

BACK STORY

If you find yourself saying why is life so hard or why am I not living my dreams? then try to go back a further into your past. You see, the reason that my life was full of lack and struggle was because it was my was my upbringing. There was no love in our house growing up.
My father's parents took me and my brother in to live with them when my parents got divorce. My brother recently asked me did I remember when my parents were together. I was so young that I only had one memory, and that was of my parents fighting, that was it. When we arrived at my grandparents' house it was obvious that they were not too happy that we were there. I remember my grandmother saying things like they are stupid, and they want amount to much in life because they came from bad blood. We never heard words like good job, how was school, and I love you. Each day was started off

with something like, you are so ugly, and no one will ever love you. We got beatings daily and I just assumed that everyone lived like that. By the time I was 18 years old I did not believe in myself and had bought in to all of the negative that had been drilled into my head. Not until I felt a glimmer of hope after reading books like "As a man thinketh" by James Allen and "The game of life by Florence Scovel Shinn". The shift started

after I started setting a few goals. I had written them a small piece of paper and had forgotten about them and was looking for something else when I found the goals in my dresser. At my amazement I had reached many of my goals that I had written. A goal is defined as the aim or object toward which an endeavor is directed and as an observable and measurable result having one or more objectives to be achieved within a more or less fixed time frame. Goal setting is a process of deciding what you want to accomplish and devising a plan to achieve the life you desire. It is also motivational technique based on the concept that practicing setting specific goals enhances performance. For goals to be effective, you must be clear about what you want in this life. It is important to pick goals that excite you and not someone else. Your goals must feel good to you for you to align with a plan for achieving them. "People with goals succeed because they know where they're going". Earl Nightingale, Motivational Speaker and Author Success is yours simply when you make the decision to get started. Starting my business was like Captain Hernan Cortes, a Spanish conquistador who instructed his soldiers to burn their ships as they went into battle. The soldiers knew that meant they would have to win or die, of course they won the battle. I quit both my jobs in which I was supervisor at both and knew that I could not go back, or it would be defeat. It is important to write down your goals. Be sure to have at least three copies of them and put them where you can see them daily. Put them on your refrigerator or bathroom mirror and carry a copy with you to glance at throughout the day.

Visualize Your Goals

Visualization is a technique that involves focusing on positive mental images to achieve particular goals. For visualization to work, a vivid picture of the desired goal must be focused on in the mind. It would be helpful to make a vision board, which is a collage of pictures that remind you of your desired goal. "Man can only receive what he sees himself receiving." _Florence Scovel Shinn, New Thought Spiritual Teacher and Metaphysical Writer

Affirmations

"Whether you think you can, or you think you can't either way you are right." Henry Ford, Founder, Ford Motor Company

To make an affirmation is to declare positively and firmly, to maintain something to be true. It is something declared to be true, a positive statement or judgment. Even if we not aware of them, we say and make affirmations every day of our lives. For example, when you say, "I hate my job," or "I don't like my mate," This is affirming an outcome that you may not want. Without thinking, you are sending these daily affirmations out into the universe. The universe reacts to what it is given, and you are giving the universe instructions for your life. You are getting what you are affirming.

Gratitude

Gratitude: The quality of being thankful; the readiness to show appreciation for and to return kindness. Thankfulness, gratefulness, or appreciation is a feeling, emotion, or attitude in acknowledgment of a benefit that one has received or will receive. "He is a wise man who does not grieve for the things which he has not but rejoices for those which he has." Epictetus, Greek Philosopher Zig Ziglar, who was an author, salesmen, and motivational speaker once said Gratitude is the healthiest of all human emotions. The more you express gratitude for what you have, the more you will have even more to express gratitude for. In the early stages of my transformation, I made a list of things to be grateful for. I started practicing daily gratitude as soon as I would wake up to start my day. The more I practiced the more my life improved. My health, finances, relationships, and business all improved. When I wrote out one of my first affirmations, I placed it on my refrigerator, bathroom mirror, and a small piece of paper. "I am so happy, and grateful now that I am making at least $ 10,000.00 a month". I would look at it every day and read it aloud. I also began to use my imagination like I did when I was a kid. The more I read it out a loud and imagine what it would feel like it got stronger and stronger.

Within a few months, of starting my business, I was making over the amount that I affirmed. On the first contract I was making at least $ 26,000 a month. Many people think that their dreams are out of reach. Many are so broken that they feel that it will not work for them, but I am a witness it works. In the process of manifesting a better life, I realized that to forgive to heal, keep an attitude of gratitude, believe that it was possible, affirm it, and imagine how it would feel once I received it.

Feed Your Mind Daily with Good Mind Food

I grow up in Alabama, which is known for its clay hills and country living. We grew corn, peas, peanuts, watermelons, collard greens, and many other vegetables and fruit. Before planting, my grandfather would hire someone to break up the land and make the soil loose. Once this process was complete, it was planting time. We would drop the seeds in the ground and add a little fertilizer. Throughout the growing process, we had to take care of the plants. We removed the grass and weeds, and we watered the plants if there was not enough rain. We also had to make sure that we picked the fruits and vegetables at the right time, or they would not be any good, because they would rot. You have to take care of your mind in the same way. Your mind is like a garden; if you let weeds and harmful insects take over, it rots away. For many years,

I believed that old paradigm that you will be just like your parents, since they are the people you were closest to in life and they had a constant influence over you. If your father was alcoholic, it was a given that you would be one. If your mother cheated on your father, you were destined to be a cheater as well. I believed this for many years, because many people I knew seemed to repeat the actions of their parents or other examples that they had growing up. However, after learning about the laws of attraction, I realized that we can choose to be the complete opposite of our parents. So, if someone tells you that you are going to be a loser, just hold onto the vision of yourself being a winner and move on to your success without feeling any malice toward that person. Keep your mind and heart pure. We must continue to take care of our minds by feeding our minds the right information: Listen to motivational speakers and read about other successful people practicing positive techniques and habits.

Motivational speaker and bestselling author Marci Shimoff said,

"If you want to be successful, practice the habits of successful people." Do not entertain the opinions of negative people who do not believe in you. Entertain the ideas of people who have goals like yourself, people who are positive and who encourage you. Learn as much as you can about vision, affirmations, gratitude, goal setting, law of attraction, and the power of your mind.

Below are a few things to remember:

_ Write down your vision or idea.

_ Use your imagination like you did when you were a child.

_ Take some kind of action that will get you closer to your vision.

_ Use self-talk by saying to yourself that you can achieve it.

_Once you have made a decision on what it is that you want, do not be afraid to act on it. "practice rather than preach. Make of your life an affirmation, defined by yourself ideas, not the negation of others.
Dare to the level of your capability then go beyond to a higher level."
_Gen Alexander Haig, Former US Secretary of State

Call to Action

If you want to change your life and get the results you want, here is your first challenge. Within the next twenty -four hours, choose an affirmation that resonates with you. Start taking steps to move yourself closer to having the life you truly want and deserve. Set goals for yourself. Repeat your affirmations daily. If you get off track, get back in the game. Be persistent. Remember to keep an attitude of gratitude.

EBS Security Inc.
904-354-4242

https://ebssecurity.com/

https://printellabankhead.com/

Representing: Nigeria

Jehovah Jireh - God My Great Provider

This is a brief story of how God's provision made a significant difference in my life for good. The full story would be very lengthy, but my objective in this short narrative is to encourage anyone who is going through challenging circumstances of life, that there is hope – as God still answers prayers and provides for His own, as He promised in His word, the Bible.

I was born to a large family in Nigeria. My parents were very loving, hardworking and did their best to provide for the family, but with their limited resources could not afford further education for them. Consequently, most of my siblings never studied beyond primary school level. Naturally speaking, my prospect of studying beyond primary school level was very slim. Without divine intervention I would not have this story to encourage you with. As God would have it, after primary education I went to Secondary school under scholarship for most of the years.

The most significant breakthrough was regarding University education. My father never considered himself as a person who could afford University education for any of his children, therefore, this was never part of his thought nor plan. One day, under intense pressure from a relative, he, either convinced or confused, asked me to apply for University on the belief that I would get scholarship following admission.

It so happened that during my first year in the university, the economy of the country went down and both the Federal and State governments suspended their scholarship schemes. One day, my father sent for me and informed me that I would have to withdraw from the University after the first year as he could not afford the fees. Although I perfectly understood his predicament, that did not remove from me a feeling of deep frustration from the prospect of having to withdraw from the University after only one year of study. From that moment, I lost interest in studying and life had no more meaning for me. In despondency, I drew up plans to commit suicide on the day I would have to withdraw from the University. It was a best kept secret that no one other than me knew about.

However, nothing is hidden from God, who had a better plan for me. One evening my friend, a more mature Christian than me, whom I used to study with asked me to accompany him to study after meals. I told him that I had no desire to study, so I returned to the hostel after meal while he went to study. A short

while later, he rushed back to my room telling me that God rebuked him for going to study alone without checking out from me - the person he called 'my son', why I was so disturbed not to study. I narrated my predicament to him.

He calmly but confidently told me to bring my books to the place we normally studied, and that when we get there, he would pray for me and God would provide. I obeyed. That night, in the open corridor where we stayed to study, he prayed for God to provide funding for me. Nothing happened after the prayers, and none of us knew how

God would provide the funding; but I had the peace of mind to resume studies. A short while after, God answered the prayer in a spectacular manner. An Oil company wrote to the University for the first time in its history, asking the Vice Chancellor to nominate three students for scholarship awards. After a series of psychometric tests, I was awarded a scholarship that covered my University education. I graduated with a First Class B.Sc (Hons) degree. Since then God has blessed my further studies with funding from various sources, including but not limited to:

* M.Sc. (in UK) – funded by a University where I was a lecturer of Engineering Geology

* PhD (in UK) – Commonwealth Scholarship

* MBA (in UK), passed with DISTINCTION – funded by employer

I currently reside in the United Kingdom – a far cry from initial prospects, had God not intervened.

The gist of this story is that God is still alive and deeply in touch with the needs of His children. He has enough resources to meet all of your needs. He is the same yesterday, today and forever more! What He did for me, He will also do for you. He is no respecter of persons. No matter your circumstances, do not lose hope and never ever contemplate suicide. Remember that no condition is permanent. What appears to be the end of the road to you today, may be just a bend in the corner. Your future is as bright as the promises in the word of God. God will help you. Take your needs to Him in prayer. Have faith in God. He will not only answer your prayers but also bless you beyond your wildest imaginations. With God all things are possible!

By: Dr. E.j. Ebuk

Representing: Oklahoma

A Winning World: The Gift of Adversity

"Out of suffering have emerged the strongest souls." -Khalil Gibran

Life is a collection of moments, and you never know which moment will change your life forever. We all have priorities, as our lives change, so do our priorities. The things that were important to us as a child grow and evolve as we age. Along the way to adulthood, these priorities often become skewed. We begin to erroneously believe that material possessions and the opinions of others are more important than they should be. Logically, we know this should not be the case, yet we are compelled and motivated by these ultimately superficial things. While in this headspace, it often takes a radical shift in perspective to bring us back to what's genuinely important in life. This message from the Universe must be obvious and undeniable. My radical shift happened while I was in the military.

While preparing to deploy, I suffered a severe spinal injury that left me paralyzed from the neck down. In an instant, I went from preparing for war on the battlefield to a war within my own body and mind. During the subsequent surgery, I died on the operating table, twice.

While the doctors saved my life, I was told that I'd never walk or use my hands again. My life went sideways. I was in a complete state of shock. I simply could not wrap my mind around the notion that I would be like this for the rest of my life. I was beside myself. The things that I kept thinking about weren't my accomplishments.

What kept coming to mind were the regrets of things I hadn't achieved. I realize that we will all have regrets in life to some extent. We are often under the romantic notion that we will live a perfectly healthy life to be 100 years old until we are lying on our deathbed, surrounded by family and close friends. But I wasn't on my deathbed. I was an otherwise healthy person who probably had another 40+ years to live in my current physical state, plenty of time to let my regret slowly eat away at me from the inside. Up to that point, I thought that I'd lived my life on my own terms and had some grand adventures. But in hindsight, I regretted not going after all the things I'd kept putting off "until tomorrow."

Lying in that bed, I had no idea what I was going to do next. My entire life had revolved around my primary objective of deploying in the military. That goal had evaporated, and now I was left without purpose or the use of my physical body. Without purpose, we look for distraction to keep us mentally, emotionally and physically occupied.

I started thinking of ways of taking my own life, but I couldn't even accomplish that in my current physical state. The things that I once thought were important became a distant memory. The education I had, the house I lived in, and car I drove mattered not. My bank account was simply a number on a screen or slip of paper that could not change my condition. Take a moment and ask yourself one question:

What would you do if you found yourself in my circumstance, what regret(s) would you harbor?

Read that statement again.

The things that are coming to mind right now, these are the things that you legitimately value. These are your Priorities, and these are the things you should start acting on this very moment. In my paralyzed state, I quickly realized that my family was a priority to me. The strong relationships I had with longtime friends was another. But there was another priority that I realized I'd overlooked. That priority was gratitude.

I realized I wasn't grateful for my health or physical abilities. I'd mistakenly taken these things for granted. In hindsight, I saw that I'd taken the time I'd been given for granted as well. Up until the time of my injury, I always assumed that I'd have "tomorrow" when I could be potentially inhaling my last breath at any moment. I tried desperately to find something, anything, to be grateful for in my paralyzed condition. I knew I should be grateful to be alive, but I felt like I wasn't really living. It felt like I was simply existing. Finally, after 3 agonizing months, I had an epiphany.

I realized that I was focusing only on myself, on my situation. I wasn't thinking about others. Once I started looking outside of me, at the positive things that my injury prevented, my mindset changed. For example, if I'd suffered this injury while I was deployed, I could have potentially put others' lives in danger. It takes many people to drag an injured man out of danger to a helicopter and fly him to safety. This means that everyone from my team to the helicopter crew and pilot of the Chinook would have been put in harm's way to save my life.

That fact became the cornerstone of gratitude upon which I could build. Slowly but surely, I began to be grateful for other things I'd taken for granted. Eventually, I was even grateful for the bed I was confined to and the room that I may never be able to leave. After 3 months, I was able to see my injury as a blessing. Once I started seeing my Adversity as a gift instead of a curse, something miraculous began to happen…the fingers on my left hand began to move ever so slightly. It wasn't much, but it was a foundation; my foundation for recovery.

After another 9 months of physical therapy and more months of occupational therapy, I was finally able to walk and function close

to normal. To this day I still have permanent nerve damage in my hands and feet. And for that, I am grateful. This impairment serves as a daily reminder of how far I have come compared to when my entire body was in the same numb condition. While distractions

are infinite, the time and ability you possess is limited. Use these precious commodities to the best of your ability while you are

still able. Take the time to realize what is truly important in your

life and act on them…now.

Your life can change in a moment as mine did, and there is precious little time to waste. Life is a collection of moments, and you never know which moment will change your life forever.

by Marcus Aurelius Anderson

Representing: Peru

The Struggle and Journey to My Winning Life By: Renato Tanamachi

When I was five my mom married a Peruvian American. She moved to America and left me behind with my great aunt. The only thing she did for me was cook for me, causing me to become independent, in a lot of respect, at age 6. I did what ever I wanted. I could walk outside, go where ever, and simply had no guidance. At age 7 my mom returned for me and we moved to Oregon with my step-dad. I now had residency and we had a pretty decent life there. My step dad was a hard worker and I always saw him in suits. It was nice to have a complete family. At age 10 my mom told me we were going to Georgia to visit her brother and we'll be back. Well, time would pass, and I wondered when we were going back to Oregon and we never did. I found out when I was 17 that my mom never intended for us to return when we'd left 7 years earlier. She had chosen to leave my step dad and just never shared her true plans.

Now in Oregon, we lived very well. I'd say we lived like an upper middle-class family. But when my mom left him, we became very poor. My step dad was about 30 years older than mom and was very established. My mom could speak no English and life away from my step dad was night and day. She hadn't had a solid a job for about 56 years and living with my uncle would end after a dispute between he and m mom. We ended up moving to Virginia where my aunt lived. We had a bed room to share and move worked 2 part time jobs to provide for us. We still never had money and our necessities couldn't be met. Looking back on it, I just don't know what she was doing with the money. I was about 12 at this point we could barely afford our necessities. It was at this age also that my mom would start talking aloud to herself. It was found that she had schizophrenia, which she still suffers from today. From age 12 to 18 mom would scream out and hallucinate. This was very stressful for me and I didn't even know what stress was at this age. Mom would wake me up every night at about 2 am and ask me questions. She would even call the police all the time, believing in her mind something had happened to me and was happening to me, but it was not so. I would have to talk to the police each time and explain, she's just having a moment. The police showing up and seeing what I was going through as a youngster, ended up being a blessing in disguise. The cops started looking out for me and at age 18, they had an event for a group of youth. They picked us up in a limousine and treated us very well. They had been keeping files on my and my situation for years, just in case something happened. They were like my guardian angels. One year earlier I'd taken a trip to Peru and I met my stepdad. I would find out after talking to him that he didn't abandoned us and he tried to get us back, but was blocked. I thought how differently my life would have been with him in our lives. Well, after back in the states, the police bless me, and mom still had episodes that I knew I'd need to get away from to live.

I told mom I was going back to Peru to visit. We had a condo there and I would choose to fix it up. Well I got a job, built extra rooms in the condo, get roommates, read and study. I was living free of stress and making life work, but knew I needed more in my life.

In 2015 I decided to get a ticket back to America about 3 or 4 years later. I would go through a few more struggles with family issues, but I'd set my heart on the military and I pressed through and got in.

There are many other pieces to the story, but what I've shared is a brief version of my journey. Though I went through much, and I needed to leave home for peace in mind, I love my mom. She did her best to provide and make a life for us. I became a better person for it and continue growing. I'm now afforded the opportunity to be a blessing to my mom and take her on travels. I'm not quite where I want to be or plan to be, but I'm serving in the military and moving forward to living the winning life I choose. No matter what we go through with work and dedication we can and will win.

Representing: Florida

The Good, The Bad, and The Ugly

We've heard it said that Life comprises of the good, the bad and the ugly. It's those good times, the bad times and yes, the ugly times that teach us, whether we like it or not. And it's those teachable moments of life that we have to be thankful for. God doesn't bring on the bad times, but he'll allow you to go through them, because we know that all things work together for good to them that love Him. There are difficult situations in life that you could never have imagined going through, let alone be thankful for. But in fact, it is those places that we grow and be transformed into the person God has called you to be. It is also in that growth and transformation that we see the mighty hand of God. It is there through the growth process that we draw nigh to God, it is there you see the grand possibilities of His plan. It simply changes you from who you used to be –to who you were always meant to be. In the process of being refined and certainly after, you find so much to be thankful for: You are thankful for the gift of time, for second chances, for the moments to come and the family to share them with. I know in my particular situation I was NO correction I AM, truly thankful for life. I awoke with no memory except what my heart knew. I affirm that the heart does have a memory, I know my heart did; when my head had no idea who anyone was, my heart did. My heart recalled the relationship I had with my Mommy, my husband, my son, my brother, my dad and daddy. What I am thankful for is that number one that I am alive after going thru situation. The situation that I am talking about is what we call in my family "my incident". On May 27th, 2017, I died twice between the hours of 7:00 pm and 9:00 pm and yet here I am ALIVE to tell my testimony. The last memory I had prior to "my incident" was getting into the ambulance and the next thing was waking up in the hospital surrounded by family a week and half later. I had no idea who I was or who the people were around me but again my heart did. For that, I am so thankful to Jesus, I am thankful for all GOD has brought me through and done for me. Hallelujah! All glory to my King!!!

By: Laura Herndon

Representing: Russia

Winning Transparency in Marriage By: Kristina Davidson

I was born and raised in south part of Russia, in a very small town located on natural underground springs. My family was my mom and my grandma. My father left us when I was a baby, still now we don't know anything about him or where he is. One thing this taught me was to never depend on any man. I learned to develop self to be able take care of kids financially, independently from man if needed. My mom was a flight attendant and had to be away from home a lot to make money to be able to support me. My granny was caregiver while mom was away. Granny was one of the top chefs in town, working part time in sanatorium restaurant. The area I'm from is famous for its health spas, and resorts called sanatoriums. Families from all over Russia come down to rejuvenate after hard working all year long. What is special about those types of resorts is that when family's check in, they are being examined by physician on site.

These physicians check the visiting family's blood. Based on the findings of the test, they prescribe certain springs, with specific chemicals in them to help patients heal. They also prescribe a specific food diet and cater to the needs of the individual that is most beneficial to his/or her health. This is what will be served by the resort as an all inclusive deal.

In Russia, Ukraine, and other former Soviet Union republics, the term sanatorium is generally used for a combination resort/recreational facility and a medical facility to provide short-term complex rest and medical services. It is like spa resorts with medical services.

My grandpa died from lung cancer when I was a little girl. I only met him once that I remember. He used to be a local writer and poet, earning small income from making articles and selling his little poetry books.
When my granny was at work, she'd drop me off to her friends and neighbors' houses until she returned from work. I rarely saw my mom. When I did see her, she dedicated little to almost no time to me. However, one thing she did do, that motivated me a lot throughout my life, is she'd read books in English to me and taught me what each word means.
One day mom inherited the house with the toilet outside. This house was built by my great grandparents right after world war 2. It was very cold in Russian. The severe winters were rough, and the outside toilet had no heater. The best part of about this toilet was that you didn't have to flush it. It went dip down into a hole in the ground. It naturally fermented into fertilizer for the plants and trees that grew around it. It is still this way till this day.
Times were very hard. I remember my mom was calling me to eat soup she'd made of water, sunflower oil, potato and a piece of onion. I'd ask her why she isn't eating, and she'd reply, "I must stretch the meal out until next day, so I can have some lunch." Often, she'd be getting paid the next afternoon and this is when she could buy food

and eat it with me. Those times made me ask questions about life and why some people have enough to eat and live and other people don't have enough.

Staying with my grandmas' friends and families taught me a lot about life and relationships. Many of which that styed with me in my mind as I grew older. I was looked for patterns in successful families, so later on in life I can recreate that for my life. I wanted change and something in me told me to see in others what I desired for my life. I found out that not only having college education determines success but also the ability to shift how we look at things.

I saw good in marriage and I saw bad. I was afforded the opportunity to see the good to take with me in my own life. It was still scary and there were times I felt, if this is what adult life is all about then I don't want to be an adult! I saw so much that I was almost discouraged about marriage life, but the good outweighed the bad.

Many things would take place in my life over time but let me fast forward. The time would come for me to go away to school and decide a major. Since I liked English language so much, I decided to study at the 5th best linguistic university in Russia. This was the school where my mom studied at before she had me. She ended up quitting because she had to take on a full-time job.

Entering wasn't easy at all. Some of my classmates from school were laughing at me when they found out about my plans to attend this university. They said, "With brains like mine, I'd never be accepted there." Truth is, I was not good at school, but if I wanted to make it to America I had to try. Students who went here, had a higher approval rate in getting visas to anywhere. I am thankful for all of my classmates who doubted be, because it made me study even harder for the entrance exam. I'd fall asleep while studying and hear their words saying, I'm not good enough to make it happen. I used that to fuel me to be more persistent and awake during my studies. At the end I passed my exams and entered the university. After that all those people who said that I won't make it, suddenly stopped talking to me completely. This is when I learnt that in life we must let go of certain friends and people in our lives.

I'd not only passed my exams, but I later became one of their best students.
As years were passing quickly, on my last years of university I was finally invited to go to the states on a visa for work and travel. Combining my money along with money from my mom and my grandmother, I was able to afford to make this happen. All I had was $250 dollars with me which would be equivalent to a one week stay of 3star motel.

Fast forwarding to meeting my husband.
One day one of the students asked me if I wanted to move it with them in apartment and share the rental cost. I loved the idea of finally having a kitchen, washer and dryer. When we moved in, I noticed she had a male friend who looked very different from all of us. He was from Jamaica. His skin appeared as a charcoal color. She said he was her boyfriend. I thought wow, that's bold to be with that guy despite of skin differences. Other roommates were making jokes about such a diversity secretly, especially when he'd sit on our black leather coach and he'd blend in with it.
Later, as time passed by, her friend with benefits decided to ask her to introduce me to him. He said he liked me, Irina said no, don't you worry about her, she is not interested in guys, she is lesbian. Which was not true. She explained later, that it was a ploy to keep him away from me and keep his focus on her. I was not even aware nor concerned with this as my focus was on work and self-establishment in America. Well, the time would come and this girl room-mate would leave. And this guy friend would keep returning to talk to me. I tried using the excuse I don't talk English, but it didn't work. He was so persistent day after day, week after week, month after month he would keep himself useful, and accountable.
So later we decided to open a business agency together to help student immigrants like myself with jobs and accommodations. One

day my friends said that this Jamaican friend of mine looking at me like he is in love with me. I said, what?! Me and this guy, he is too dark. No never will I be with a such dark guy like him. Well, He became my HUSBAND, a few years later. That lesson taught me NEVER SAY NEVER!!! This would not only be a shock to those we knew, but to my mother. I'll go into that story in a future book.

I remember our first date and touching his hand. I felt on his dark skin, trying to see if his skin would feel different than mine, because in Russia we don't have that dark-skinned people. And when I felt that his skin was just like mine, I even spoke it to him. OMG look your skin feels just like mine. He was laughing so hard, he said no one ever was feeling his skin like that. To me it was all experimental.
I couldn't believe that such a big difference in skin color could still feel the same. We made it through these comical times and where mom was hesitant, she fell in love with how he loved me and accepted the relationship no matter what the skin color was.

Now we have been married for 10 exciting years with 2 beautiful sun tan caramel children who my mom loves to the moon and back. We created a new race "Russmaicans", that's Russia and Jamaican combined. I expose them to both cultures as much as I can. Dealing with such different, diverse cultures was exciting and challenging. We are both in the real estate business. Going through the challenges in life now is more exciting to me than before, because now I have a power of getting any information necessary immediately thru internet.   Transparency
Now what I'm about to share about my relationship many wouldn't agree, but it's my belief and has kept me winning in my marriage and family life. This is where most of couple either look for counseling either braking up and go separate ways or working it out to keep their families together. I've gone through all the emotions one could imagine. This is real, and this happens often, but most won't talk about it. The biggest thing was wondering why my

husband was interested in other women and how could I put a stop to it. I was determined to not give up on my marriage. After trying different approaches and bumping into a brick wall, I did research and found out that male species have a different type of nature than women. It's the same they just have different approaches. It all comes from embedded human instincts. The idea of just accepting this didn't work for me. I can't just be aware my husband is cheating, and I remain quiet. I don't want to pretend, I don't want to divorce and break marriage nuptials. So, I gave my husband room and privilege to open up to me freely with peace and searching a solution. It worked. He admitted it to me. As he shared why I realized that I needed to become his best friend not another woman. I must be his everything not another. Now not to shift the blame from his wrong choices, but to view it through different eyes to help save my family and do what had to be done to keep it. I didn't want to be a single mom. So, making an unconventional move, I invited her to eat with us instead. She got scared and didn't come in. I said oh well... maybe next time then.... Then I hear my husband talking to her often, I thought ok I have a choice now either get upset with him or pretend that I don't know anything. Well by now you must know, I wasn't going to be the quiet mouse running and hiding. I made another conventional move and instead I decided to acknowledge, and encourage the phone conversations like that, my husband loved it, now he can have of none judgmental freedom to be that super hero that strong shoulder for her, I decided he better let him do it in front of me then somewhere else I can have better awareness and more control over situation. Again, most would say, bad move, but no, it worked in my favor. Now to say I didn't go through moments of insecurity and thinking I'm not enough, I'd be lying. But the fact that I took that stand I took is proof that if you want something bad enough, you'll fight to win. There are a lot of blanks I'll fill in in a soon coming book, but as of Today, I have my husband. We're not perfect, yet we are happy with our family, and I'm not a single mother, but a happy wife and mother to our children.

Representing: Florida

Fight to Win

"Fight to win" is the message and the moral of my story. I've always thought that Fighting to win was an ingrained or natural inclination. I never thought that fighting to win was something that needed to be taught or encouraged. I believed that Fighting to win was a part of a human's most powerful survival instinct. As if fighting to win was some sort of default setting in our personal programming. Yet, there are many people in this world who are fighting battles daily without any intention of winning. There are even people who commit spiritual suicide by deliberately self-sabotaging any hope of victory but Why?
What's stopping these people from putting forth a winning effort? Some people won't give winning efforts because they don't think their battles can be won. So, they chose to give up and lose by default.

In our Daily lives, we are constantly fighting our own personal battles. Battles that are as unique as a fingerprint. Personal battles can happen to anyone in all areas of our life with various combinations and levels of intensity. These battles usually take place in three main area: our minds, our bodies, and our spirit. When life's battles are happening simultaneously in all three those main areas, life can get very tough. But if we allow personal battles to overwhelm us with stress and worry. The littlest things seem massive and the simplest problems seem complex. Our imagination can skew our visions of future. But no matter the variation, combination or intensity of battle, we must still fight and fight to win.

> Because, somewhere in the world right now, there are people who have been convinced that they can't win their personal battles and as result, they are ready to give up and quit fighting a battle that could be well within their grasp. Maybe you know a person in this situation. Someone on the verge of forfeiting their battle because the odds of winning seemed insurmountable. Maybe they feel as if they have nothing to fight for or they have nothing to fight with or they just feel like they are fighting all alone... if this is you then my message to you is: continue to fight and fight to win.

> We must realize that even thought it might not always be obvious, the win we're fighting for is never just for ourselves. Sometimes our wins can serve as the motivation and momentum for other's faith. It starts a faith cycle. Faith creates motivation. Motivation creates momentum. Momentum create movement and it becomes a move of faith So, when it seems like you can't get thing moving, you can't seem build any momentum, focus on your faith and fight to win. Because when we fight to win, we are moving by faith.

By: Dr.Bj Fletcher

Representing: Florida

"Surviving Against the Odds" By:
Victoria R. Blackman

It was always difficult for me to dress out for gym class, to wear a swim suit or a high-rise waisted blouse. These low self-confidences stimmed from my childhood burns I received at age six. The burns covered over 85 percent of my body, which included my face, my entire stomach, thighs, arms, and hands.

My mother left my two siblings and me home from one day as she needed to go grocery shopping. Before she left the house, she had me to put the latch on the screened door, which I did. Soon after mother out of sight I went into the kitchen to turn on the pilot lit oven. I recall this moment just as if it happened yesterday. Knowing now as an adult, I waited too long to attempt to lite the oven. As I proceeded to strike the first match, a wind from nowhere blow out the match fire. I struck the second match and another wind blow out the match fire. I struck the third match and a sparkle from the match fall onto my French Poodle wool skirt. As I attempted to blew out the sparkle, a fire blazed up. Knowing now as an adult what happened, I apparently waited too long to lite the gas oven by then the gas had already accumulated in the air and after blowing on the sparkle, once the air and gas combusted it ignited causing the fire.

Remember now, my mother made sure I locked the porch screened door before she left the house. Our kitchen was on the back end of the house. Running to the front door, I saw that it was unlocked allowing me to run straight out of it. I stood on the front porch screaming until I caught the attention of a Caucasian man riding on a tractor. The man had just put a pile of dirt in our front yard when he saw me on fire, he threw the tractor in gear, jumped down from it ran to me picking me up with his bare hands as I continued to burn. This man saw no Black or White child. He saw a child on fire needing his help. The way he picked me up, he had to have received deep burns in his hands and arms. That is how close he

held me to him. Lord Jesus! I believe he suffered getting to sleep that night after witnessing such horrific ordeal.

After multiple plastic surgeries, I was able to return back to school repeating the first grade because of the burn incident. So, I am back in school only to face cruel remarks and name calling from the other children. Many times, the name calling came from my siblings as well. They had all kinds of names for me that my mother did not name me. Nevertheless, I never said anything back to the other children or to my siblings. The name calling would continue throughout high school. Of course, the name calling was even harsher at this level mainly because the children are now older, much wiser, and smarter with their choice of words. During the latter part of high school, I begin to search for this man whom I would later call my angel because he truly rescued and saved my life, but to no avail. Again, racism was very high in Jacksonville, FL. (my home town) back in the 60's but this man who (if he is still alive) would be about my father's age somewhere in his late 80's today. I would still love to meet him just to say thank you, and I love you for being my hero in such a troubled racial time in the 60's. If I do not see you in this walk of life, I hope you will be there in heaven when I get there.

At age 21, I met and married my first husband, which that marriage lasted almost 15 years but was very abusive. The marriage would end with much disappointment, hurt, anger, and sadness, which would later lead to depression. The depression didn't last long though because one year later I met and married my second and again this marriage was worse than the first. I felt this guy loved his mother and God so surely, he would love me...he was an elder and his mother was the pastor and founder in the same church where we met. Again, this was another disappointing failed marriage and I just knew this would be the last time marring would happen for me. I was too hurt to even think about tying the knot every again. The Lord had a different plan for my personal life than I had for myself. The pain of loneliness was so deep in my flesh that I said to God "God if you don't help me, I am going to help myself by going out to meet someone for sexual healing. Yeah, right! A little over three months after I was on my way to work and need to stop for gas. While gassing up my car, I heard someone say to me "can I pump that gas for you?" I quickly looked at the man and responded, "no thank you I'm just about done." Then he said, "can I pay for it for you?" I responded, "it's already on my card and paid for." He walked toward me saying, Victoria, you don't know me? I responded saying "I'm sorry, am I to know you?" he said I know your brother—I know your sisters—and named them all. To my surprise, the man was my high

school secret admirer. He told me that he always had a crush on me since we were small in middle school and liked him as well, but we never told each other.

Well, three months passed by and we had no contact until a friend invited me to her husband's birthday party. As I walked in the door at the party, I was greeted by Janet who proceeded to ask if I knew the man standing about 20 feet from us, I stated no I do not know him. Janet said that's Ron from Grand Park. Ron was the man that I met at the service station three months ago and Grand Park is the community where we all grew up. At the end of the night Ron gave me all his contact information for me to call him. I did not call him though. It wasn't until Janet called me months later to inform me that Ron was in the hospital. As destiny would have it, I called his hospital room to check on him and that conversation lead us to a dating relationship months later. Short story, Ron proposed to me at my mother's house on Christmas day (in Grand Park.)

One night I invited Ron over for dinner, when he arrived, I greeted him at the door wearing a two-piece sleepwear outfit and pump shoes. I did this because I needed to make sure I was not opening another door for a failed marriage, as this would be the third marriage for me. I said to Ron "is this what you want for the rest of your life (referring to the burn scares on my body.) Ron looked at me and my body with deep concern. He walked toward me, knelt down and kissed all the scars on my body, as he said to me "baby you don't need to do this. I love you and everything about you inside and out. It was at that point that I felt beautiful for the very first time and all the shamefacedness dissipated concerning my scared body and brokenness. You see even though I was previously married, I never felt pretty or totally accepted the way Ron made me feel. This man truly brought out the best in me to see me for who I am, which is wonderfully and fearfully made by God. I am an original. There is nothing my husband would not do for me. I work if I choose to not that I have to. Yes, we have disagreements, but we learn how to overcome the obstacles we face by communicating our feelings whether good or bad. We know that we overcomer come the devil by the blood of the Lamb and every word of testimony.

Representing: Puerto Rico

Manny Garcia Story

Life is made up of moments, like scenes in a movie. Some of those "moments" you'll always remember as being significant, even if you didn't know why at the time. One of those extended moments for me, happened while attending Catholic School in New York City at the age of nine.

It was the middle of a typical lunch day, and I was sitting with my best buddy Patrick. Patrick was a stocky, happy and funny kid with black hair and blue eyes. He told me once he was Irish which was surreal because, on Saint Patty's day, March 27th of 1983 one of those "moments" would show up unforgettably.

While chowing down on some Mac & Cheese, a hotdog and some corn, I was staring at the picture of a little girl on the front of my chocolate milk carton. Above her image were the words "MISSING." I vaguely remember some thoughts that passed through my mind about her – how old she might be, how she went missing or how sad her family was to have lost her. But mostly I was thinking about finishing lunch and heading out of the cafeteria to play during recess.

Suddenly Patrick leaned over and tapped me on the shoulder, with a big grin on his face.

"Hey Manny, why are you on my milk carton?" he said as he showed me his carton. I looked at the carton and in amazement, staring back at me was this kid who looked just like a younger me – weird. He even had a similar name – Manuel Garcia. I laughed, and we both shook our heads for a moment, then Patrick went back to his lunch.

I continued staring at the side of his carton, and my amusement turned to confusion. Was that kid me? And if it was, when did I go missing? I couldn't understand why a younger me, would be on the side of a milk carton. I remember thinking, how was it possible to be missing if I lived with my dad?

After we finished our lunch, Patrick tossed the remains of his meal away, along with his carton of milk. I followed behind him and quickly snatched the small empty carton from the trash, folded it and put it in my back pocket.

Throughout the day, I kept reaching into my pocket to look at the picture on the milk carton. At one point I remember locking myself in the bathroom of my babysitter's house after school ended, the more I looked at the picture, the worse I felt. By the time my dad came to collect me after work, my unease had grown to dread.

As soon as we got home, I told my dad that I thought I must be in big trouble. His face immediately grew stern, and he asked me what had happened. I pulled out the milk carton from my pocket and showed it to him. To this day I still remember the look on his face. I've never seen a man's eyes get that big before or since that day.

Then he gave a little nervous laugh and said not to worry, "it must be a mistake" he said. He offered me some chocolate milk and a peanut butter jelly sandwich. Later, when he put me to bed, everything seemed completely normal.

The very next morning, my dad told me to get in the car, and before I knew it, we were headed towards Miami with some of our belongings. For a while, I didn't say anything, but then I asked my dad why we were leaving. I knew it must be because of the milk carton, but I couldn't understand why. After all, he'd said I'd done nothing wrong.

My dad had a nervous look on his face; he seemed VERY unhappy! Then he slowly explained that there were some bad people after us and he had to keep me safe. I wasn't sure what to say and before I could ask why, he mentioned that on our way to Miami we would be going through the south side of Orlando. He reminded me that was where Mickey Mouse lived and that we could visit him if I liked. I was so excited by his offer and the thought of seeing the great mouse, I momentarily forgot about the "bad people" who were after us.

Disney was great, but after the initial excitement had faded, I began to look around at the other families there. I kept seeing moms and dads holding hands with their children hanging onto them. I envied those kids, and I wanted to be just like them, visiting Disney with both my parents. Unfortunately, I didn't live with both parents, and I hadn't seen my mom for a long time.

Let me give you a bit of backstory. In my early years, we all lived together as a family in Orlando with my father. But my father was obsessed with music, and my mother divorced him after coming home one night early from work and catching him beating my sisters because they failed to master their piano lessons.

My mother fled with us to Puerto Rico, seeking refuge with her sister and because of my youth, the memory of those early years eventually became a blur to me. My mother tried to shield us from how obsessed and enraged my father became because of her rejection and the subsequent divorce. He followed us to Puerto Rico and for years would periodically appear at my aunt's home with machetes and knives, scraping them on the sidewalk or chain link fence and threatening to kill us all if my mother refused to remarry him. My aunt would call the police, and he would disappear for a while before showing up again unannounced and repeating the same behavior. He was relentless.

One day, my sister was involved in a severe accident. She'd been walking down a street with her best friend when they suddenly saw a car lose control and hurtled towards them. My sister instinctively pushed her friend out of the way and saved her life. It was a brave thing to do; but as a result, ended losing her arm when the bumper of the vehicle smashed her arm against a steel utility box which was near them.

The paramedics rushed my sister to the hospital, and the whole family gathered around, in shock, desperately worried. In the middle of the chaos, my father showed up at the

hospital; my family consumed with grief and fear for my sister temporarily forgot the potential threat he posed.

On that very day at the hospital, while all eyes were understandably on my sister, my dad for once behaved calmly and with care. He offered to take me to McDonald's to grab something to eat and told my mother he would bring me soon after. My mother was beside herself with anxiety and heavily medicated, and in her confused state, agreed. It would be the last time she saw me and the final day I would spend living in Puerto Rico.

So, the reason I saw my face on a milk carton was that my mother was desperately searching for me after my abduction. But it wouldn't be until my father died in a tragic motorcycle accident when I was eleven that she would see me again.

These early experiences shaped me in many ways, not least that they are a core part of the reason I became the type of leader I am today. Growing up with my father was intense. He was a perfectionist and would punish me harshly if I ever performed anything with less than a perfect outcome. The fear of being punished came at the expense of making more mistakes and an avalanche of emotional distress for both of us.

I grew up in an environment where I honestly felt that I was never good enough. I was always being scrutinized and criticized for my lack of performance, whether it was in academics or music. As you can imagine, living in this type of environment was very toxic, but it taught me some powerful lessons over time.

After my father died, I spent a lot of time feeling lost, depressed and confused. I was lucky enough however to find mentors who showed me how to transform some of my childhood experiences into growth opportunities. These growth opportunities lead me to a definite purpose for my existence as I explored adulthood. One of these mentors was Don Francisco, a science teacher, and astrologer in Puerto Rico. He knew my family and was a witness to my abduction.

After my father passed away, I was reunited with my mother and went back to live with her in Puerto Rico. Don Francisco lived three houses down from my aunt's house, a few blocks away from my mother's home. When visiting my aunt, I would notice that he would watch me from a distance at times. We would greet each-other from time-totime, but we never indeed engaged in any meaningful conversation until one late evening when I was sixteen.

On that evening, while walking fast and lost in an emotional state of distress, I passed by Don Francisco's home as he worked on his car and he called me over. I was angry and combative, but he looked at me and calmly said that he was sorry about my father. Then he said, "I can only imagine what you've been through and for that, I'm very sorry."

It wasn't so much what he said but how he said it. For the first time in as long as I could remember, I broke down into tears. I could barely breathe as I gasped for air, sobbing hysterically. Part of me was confused and had no clue what was happening, why I was crying this way in front of a man I barely knew, but I could no longer hold in my emotions.

After a few minutes, I calmed down and felt a massive surge of emotional relief. I had never allowed myself to feel emotion like that since my dad passed. I'd grown to believe that being controlled and stern all the time had made me less vulnerable, causing me the least amount of pain. Looking back, I realized that as a teenager, I'd become "living dead," a Zombie to the emotions within me.

After talking for a while that evening, I realized how much Don Francisco knew about my family. He invited me to visit with him whenever I wished. I didn't have an influential father figure at the time, so I accepted his offer and would visit with him occasionally. For the next few years, I began to learn many lessons from his mature perspective, many of which I still use. They are with me now as part of my emotional and intellectual toolbox.

One fundamental lesson Don Francisco taught me was his explanation of how everything in life comes with an opportunity to learn something either negative or positive from it. As a defiant sixteen year old, this didn't make much sense to me at the time, but it did plant a seed. A seed that later grew into a belief as I transitioned from a teenager to an adult that would help me make wiser life choices by learning from my mistakes. This same lesson was the cure that allowed me to heal emotionally from my childhood trauma and understand that there can be some excellent things to learn from most situations that occur in life.

Eventually, I was able to flush away the negative traits I had picked up from my father and built upon the good qualities he did have instead. Things like, always giving your best no matter what you do, or to never quit the pursuit of your goals regardless of how many challenges and pain you may face.

I also learned that people's weaknesses or failures could become an avenue to building strength by doing the complete opposite. For instance, instead of using words to criticize people negatively or destructively that could otherwise crush their spirit, as I once felt by my father; you could instead use your words to coach, encourage and build people up by increasing their confidence, shortening their learning curve and helping them to be more productive.

Some life lessons came about by avoiding the same traps we witnessed others doing which led them to massive failure and pain. However, the best lessons usually come from our most painful personal life experiences. My father wasn't an evil man; it was his false beliefs that led to his anger, as he never learned how to manage his emotions. He had his good traits, just like anyone else. But for me, it was his negative traits that had the most impact as I determined never to be like him. I never wanted my children to experience the negative characteristics that my father caused me to suffer. Because of this, the most significant gift I received from my dad was a crystalclear model of how not to behave. For that gift, I am genuinely grateful.

I've shared my story with you because it has given me a perspective on life leadership. We all lead someone, our children, spouses, friends, coworkers, etc. Being able to live a

balanced life focused on bringing value-based contributions onto others, indeed is the difference maker. You see as a life leader; you have the same opportunity to either be like my father to crush and dishearten people with your words and actions or to use your leadership power to develop and bring value onto others. The way you choose to interact with other people, how you build them up or break them down, will directly impact their effectiveness and your overall success in life.

I've been blessed to learn from some very amazing people who have inspired and taught me leadership secrets which have given me the edge to position myself as an influential leader within world-class companies. These same companies have served as a growth vehicle for me to gain experience working in the United States and Asia, where I've built teams responsible for over a Billion dollars in sales revenues. These same secrets applied in my own companies have allowed me to build organizations with millions of dollars in sales, the opportunity travel around the world and experience different cultures as well as earn the freedom of time and financial reward to do what I want when I want. 1

I am forever grateful to all my mentors who have changed my life, and now I would like to "Pay-it-Forward" by assuming the responsibility of sharing what I've learned with you.

To learn more about Manny Garcia and here more life stories, I invite you to visit and meet with me online at the following website. Website: www.mannygarciaonline.com

Representing: The Netherlands

Journey to Healing

Shermanda, I'm very honored to be part of your life and your invitation to take part of your book. I hope to inspire those reading who also have many challenges in their lives or with their beloved ones.

First, I'm very blessed with my husband John and my son Bodhi. I've had a lot of health issues that have impacted my life and the lives of those close to me, from family to friends.

My issues started on December 31th 1999, with lifting up my neighbor's kid. At first, the same and that I'd be sore for a little time. No big deal. Throughout the years my health issues began getting worse instead of getting better.

I began writing letters to clinics for different kinds of treatments. Their answer was, "We can't help you." This was a very depressing and frustrating time, as I couldn't find help. I tried every type of physiotherapy. That didn't work out. Pain clinics, needles in my back, you name it, I was trying it. Some surgeons didn't want to operate me. In one year, I had over 40+ visits for medical reasons. Well, I stopped counting. I got around with a walking stick for a while.

I had so much pain and I'd been put on a lot of medicine. This only caused more issues as I became addicted to Morphine. I took 90 mg a day for several years. I had migraine attacks every week and I had a "hanging" neck. I couldn't even hold my head for a while. Sitting in a chair wasn't possible. I grew to love my Fat Boy recliner as my favorite "chair" for years. Getting in it wasn't that much of a problem, but it was very comical to see me getting up out of the chair. The experience was written all over my face every time. I had to roll over, get on my knees, hold on to a chair, and little by little I could stand straight again. Over the years we bought different beds. I also slept on an airbed in our living room at one point.

I'd lost my freedom to get up and go like normal people. I felt sometimes very isolated and alone. But, through it all, I was very blessed to stay at home with Bodhi.

When this all started Bodhi was 1 years old and went through to age 5 years old. I felt I was a bad mum. I couldn't play that much with him. I couldn't lift him up. Going outside was very difficult because I was really afraid that something could happen to him. I wasn't allowed to drive a car. I couldn't cycle. So, every day I walked him to school. Our walk was around 16 km a day. All together it took me a few hours.

Even through the pain, we went away for holidays, amusements parks, visiting family and friends, weddings, birthdays, reunions, etc. As much as I could, I'd participate. Making pancakes for the kids at school was a joy as well. It cheered me up. It took an awful lot of energy and caused great pain, but I'd do it. This would oftentimes take me a week or more to "recover". It was worth it. Also, I was participating in a pop choir for a few years during this time. Singing was a wonderful medicine.

Finally, the doctors realized I needed surgery. Finding a cure and just the right surgical procedure hasn't' been easy. Within 16 years, I had 3 surgeries for we now know were hernias. Finally, after 14 years someone told me I could get another surgery for blocking my vertebrae's. My fourth surgery. I had to walk around with a plaster band to see if the surgery would work out for me. Lucky me, it did. In April 2015, I finally made it to the operating room. I was luckier during the surgery because normally they don't operate if there's no space left between the vertebrae. Which there was no space left between mine after all these years. It was a blessing that I had no new MRI scan. There would have been no hope for me if one had been done right before the surgery.

The first 3 months after surgery, I wasn't allowed to stoop. I had to eat straight up for a while. I had to practice and learn again to sit down. Then the magic words were said, "I may start training again." This was music to my ears. Every day I went to the sport school. I started with 10 mins., training every day. The few increased the work out time to 15 mins. every day. Which eventually built up to a full hour training.

I was really upset in the beginning as I though about, why nobody told me for decades now there was another option for me to solve my problem. Naturally one would think about such things, but I am thankful. I let go and that thought is gone.

I had one more surgery to go in 2016. I had a hump (bone), which was sitting at the back of my head, removed. After this surgery I had no more migraines and neck issues. Looking back on it, I was truly thankful to have great help from a lot people around me, during my years of medical issues. Letting go of my independence wasn't easy and I had no choice. When you sit back and reflect, I realized and thought of the fact that there are many people dealing with even greater issues than mine. Although, 2 new hernia's have developed, I will beat it again. Hopefully in a shorter period of time. Truth is 2017/2018 have been great years. No more issues. Having fun with my family. Working now together with my husband in our company. I'm truly having fun times with our wonderful son Bodhi.

I can only advice you from my point of view. If you feel the slightest changes in your body and you know something is going on, Don't

Wait! Don't let doctors tell you fairytales. Believe in yourself and take action A.S.A.P.!

Enjoy the beautiful moments as much as possible, despite what you're going through, with your beloved ones and dearest friends.

Wishing you all the best!

Greetings from the Netherlands,

Ilonka van Putten-Heijster

Representing: Alabama

Overcoming Childhood Scars

The problem started when I was about 8 to 9 years old, my mother left the family and moved to Jacksonville, Florida. I had a feeling that things were over between them. They fought all the time. I didn't want to believe that it was over between them, but it was. I noticed that my mother and my father's relationship with one another was growing apart just by the way they acted around each other. The conversations between them became shorter and their affection for one another began to fade. It looked like the nights were very difficult, the atmosphere was so bad in the house, and you could cut it with a knife. It was hard to deal with the pain of seeing all that. I knew the family was falling apart. I wondered what next, what's going on. When my mother said that she was getting a divorce from my dad, it was painful. I didn't know what to do next because I was so young. I could not think about who was going to take us. I feel like it is better for the children, for parents to get separated rather than to live in a bad atmosphere with conflict, than with the parents who stay together for the children. When one chapter closes you have got to move to the next one. Every divorce will affect the children. The initial reaction is one of shock, sadness, frustration, anger, or worry. But children also can better themselves if you can cope with stress and many become flexible.

There were four of us and two went with my Father and two went with my Mother. I wonder how my Mother felt at that moment. We never talked about it again. In the end God takes care of all that so, you should not hold anything, because, "vengeance is mine saith the Lord I will repay." My Father took us to our grandparents and put us in a bad situation. People do not realize that grandparents can play a vital role in a grandchild's life. They provide support, kindness, laughter, and all kinds of love and happiness. When one of your grandparents is struggling with alcoholism, all of this can change. Many people have good intentions, but an alcoholic grandparent can really be a sad case, and toxic to their grandchild or to any one, including themselves. It may cause other problems like hatred, violence, beating, and other things that I had to go through; troubling things that I would rather not talk about. I think that what happened was because my grandmother hated my mother and took it out on us. You should realize that it will bring problems behind all the abuse and hurt. Many times, the things that they do to you will make you want to do the same things to other people around you.

"The scars of child abuse linger in the bodies of victims long after they have grown up, manifesting in physical symptoms that hint at their trauma," an Australian Psychiatrist, Dr. Michelle Atchison told delegates at the Royal Australian College of Physicians Congress in Adelaide this month. There is something about childhood trauma that make you weaker to illness later on in life, independent of coping with problems like mental problems and sexual addiction. The pain and illness can be real or imagined where psychological distress presents as physical symptoms. He said I had a lot of verbal abuse often involving put downs and name calling, which makes the victim feel like nobody loves them. The person that abuses tries to make you think that it is not happening, it is not real; that it is all in your head. Verbal abuse is dangerous because it is often not easily recognized as abuse. It can make you inflect severe damage to yourself and cause your selfesteem and your self-worth to be very low.

First of all, counselors will evaluate your level of depression along with the issues that are getting you depressed. Through talk therapy, your counselor will be able to extract your pain points, from those events you talk, to help you work through feeling depressed to overcoming. Slowly, counseling will help you clear your mind. When I started going to counseling, I got better day by day.

In life something happens, and you can't get over all of the pain. I could not help myself. The things that cross your mind like, a) I am damaged, b) I am worthless, c) There is no hope, d) I cannot make things better e) I am unlovable f) I am bad g) The world is not a safe place and so on. I met with a counselor and my life began to change overnight. I always believed in the healing power of talking to someone about your problems, but to go through the therapeutic process myself, it changed my life forever. It showed me I wanted to dedicate my life to helping others, just as I had been helped myself. In that short period of time, she gave me coping skills to overcome recent losses or transition difficulties. You started out with working on loving yourself and relying on a support team, because it is the key to recovery.

After having a life of pain, rejection, and being abandoned by birth parents, which caused me to have feel great grief and loss, I was finally being set free. There are times when these feelings surface and sooner or later they do, that you must remind yourself of the talks you had with your therapist. There are feelings of loss and no hope accompanied by a damaged sense of self-esteem. There is an understandable tendency to think that something must be wrong with me for my birth mother to give me away. It must be understood, that these feelings and thoughts are unrelated to the amount of love and support received from the adoptive parents and family. Guilt will be accompanied by loss and grief because the adopted people in my case treated me bad as well. They hurt me, betrayed me, hated my mother but I was left with them to raise me. Feelings of Why me? Why am I so different than other people that are around me?

Despite encouragement, I was not ready to go forward in life. Long discussions in therapy never revealed what I feared. According to the great psychologist, Eric Erikson, adolescence involves a search for self-identity. While this search is difficult for most teenagers, parents and family have no idea their genetic background hurts, but there is a need to help yourself and oftentimes you can't do it alone.

As messed up as I was, God called me to be one of his children. At one time I had so many problems I felt like I had no hope at all. I could not come unless God drew me to him. From a young age I was serious to find what is the meaning of life. It took some time before I got to God. The turning point took place when I was fifteen years of age. I had so many problems that I was feeling miserable and didn't think that I had a real purpose to live. I believed that God is real, but I did not know who he was. I knew something was missing in my life. I felt like it was better to die than to live in this terrible world. The night when I got saved (accepted Christ in my heart), one of the greatest evangelists of that day and time was running a revival service at our church. I gave my life to God and all the pain and hatred for humanity went away. The power of God went through my body. Something like an electric shock of power and warmth went through my body like a wave. It was power but at the time it was gentle. It was so warm to me. Yes, the power of the Holy Ghost moved over me. It looked like a new world. The world looked different, people looked different, and everything was different; including me. I began to speak in tongues as the Spirit gave me the utterance. I was changed.

I love what counseling can do for a person. Counseling typically works one-on-one. The help uncovers the source of stress, pain, resentment, frustration etc. in a person's life. I wrote a book about comprehensive Christian counseling study. Dr. Gary Collins uniquely explains that one of the things that counselors do is that we assist people, so they can get unstuck. The Christian counselors help them to improve their mindset. The aim of Christian counseling is to help people regain a sense of hope for their life that is found in Jesus Christ.

Christian counselors believe that at the core of what they do is to help others achieve a better understanding of themselves and God which is rooted in the Holy Spirit's conviction. There is no distinction at this directory between the professional Christian therapist and the professional therapist who is a practicing Christian. We have also permitted the listings of credentialed pastoral counselors. I believe that the world counselor can help you, but the greatest help comes from the Lord. How does psychology work with Christian counseling? Many times, psychology and Christianity often bump heads and are at odds with each other. I really believe that some Christians especially those involved in Bible counseling believe the Bible contains all that is necessary to overcome any issue. I believe that the Bible alone is our life manual. Yes, we have Christians believing that a person's struggles are primarily spiritual, and that God alone can heal. On the other hand, secular psychologist claim biological or developmental disruptions are the issue and that that man can fix himself. So, I wrote about how I felt about Christian counseling. Biblical counseling is a form of counseling that relies solely on scripture and the power of the Holy Spirit to achieve the best results. To me it is important for people to not be quiet about our Faith as we counsel with the person's conviction. One of the saddest situations is when people have gotten themselves stuck in uncomfortable places; depression, anxiety, interpersonal turmoil, guilt etc. Remember that our goal is to set a person free from their problem. I found out that psychology and Christianity are totally incompatible. It is an oxymoron. Because Psychology has its roots in ancient philosophers like Socrates, Aristotle, and Plato, they are not worshippers of the true and living God. My book tells of the power of Christian counseling. It is my experience that I share with conviction. When I walked into that church that evening, with feelings of hopelessness and just not wanting to live, I had no idea God had prepared a savior for me, to mend my broken heart and His name is Jesus. I'm have my doctorate in Christian counseling because of that change in my life and heart that took place the great night. I wanted to live and now I'm helping others live too.

EDUCATION

MAY1980 DIPLOMA, SULLIGENT HIGH SCHOOL 1998-1999, SCHOOL OF SCHOOL BIRMINGHAM, AL APRIL2005 ASSOCIATES, JACKSONVILLE THEOLOGICAL SEMINARY

APRIL2006

BACHELOR'S IN MINISTRY IN CHRISTIAN COUNSELING, JACKSONVILLE THEOLOGICAL

SEMINARY

DECEMBER 2007

MASTER'S IN MINISTRY IN CHRISTIAN COUNSELING, JACKSONVILLE THEOLOGICAL

SEMINARY

MAY 2008

DOCTORATE IN THEOLOGY, JACKSONVILLE THEOLOGICAL SEMINARY

MAY 2018

PHD IN PHILOSOPHY IN CLINICAL CHRISTIAN COUNSELING, JACKSONVILLE

THEOLOGICAL SEMINARY

PREACHED FOR 40 YEARS IN THE CHURCH OF GOD IN CHRIST DISTRICT SUPERINTNDENT OVER 5 CHURCHES IN THE STATE OF ALABAMA

Contact:
https://www.psychologytoday.com/us/therapists/joemackbankhead-sulligent-al/414099

Spirituality and Mindfulness

SOON RELEASED BOOK

By Joe Bankhead

Representing: California

A Journey Towards Overcoming My Greatest Obstacle

Today, speaking in public is a powerful passion of mine. I just simply love to speak and deliver my message as well as teaching. In fact, I can't get enough. I cannot imagine not being able to speak in public. And yet it wasn't always this way.

I want to take you on a short journey through my own life and my own experiences and the beliefs that I had at one time. Beliefs are the catalyst that directs our behavior, how we see ourselves, and so much more. Beliefs are part of the underlying aspects of our unconscious mind. In my life I was being guided by those beliefs. This was a belief system that was not optimal. I would say it was less than even the lowest part of what I can imagine. My belief system or BS was completely messed up. I would surmise many people reading this would have the same understanding regarding their belief system, right?

Let me I'll begin. I can remember early in my life when my mother was teaching me Kendo. At this time, I was about 18 months old. Here is the reason she started me on this journey of being a warrior: I had been sitting in the middle of the yard and there was this anthill. Like any toddler or a baby or whatever I was sitting in the middle of the yard and ants started crawling all over me. I don't know if I was bitten (as I don't recall the details) I do know that my mom noticed that I was crying. She saw the ants and then she grabbed the garden hose and started spraying me from head to toe. Then she took me into the bathroom (to get any other ants off of me) and into the tub and started soaking me in the bathtub. Being that young I was terrified of what was happening. I start seeing ants and things floating in the water. Because they were floating, I developed a fear of water. I was even scared of taking a bath for months and years after the initial incident. Yes, I had a strong memory. Memories that are formed around a strong emotional incident tends to be remembered. My mother wanted me to learn to become stronger. And that came from studying the Martial Arts of kendo.

From there I started studying other Martial Arts. While living in Okinawa, as a child, I studied Goju-Ryu karate for three years. Martial Arts became of way of life for me and a part of everything I did. Even when I started school and when I wasn't very effective or smart, The Martial Arts was my saving grace.

And believe you me I'll be gosh really needed that kind of regiment to help me develop a better mindset. I had to deal with my father and both his verbal abuse and his physical abuse. Had my first broken nose from him I had whippings on bare skin with a thin belt which lead to bleeding on my skin. And I became really terrified I had a bad stuttering problem. I am my father called me stupid and retarded. And because I installed the belief system into me, I really come to believe that I really was stupid and retarded. I also suffered from PostTraumatic Stress Disorder (PTSD) as a child.

This was carried into to my life where I was diagnosed with being mentally retarded after taking an IQ test at the age of 5 1/2. I had a score of 70.

My diagnostic label was that of a moron. I carried that label for many years and it wasn't even the external parts of my life that was affected. It was the internal beliefs that I had and which I intended to live up to that label.

I also developed a stuttering which stayed with me for a long time. That affected my self-esteem is well. I think one thing that stopped me from being able to speak up was the stuttering, my lack of selfconfidence and the idea or belief that I was basically stupid.

I had a fear of my father too. I remember trying to hide from him whenever he came home. Many times, he would be away for a couple of years. Those years that he was away, was a blessing.

The stuttering stayed with me for many years. I could perform in physical activities such as in sports. I played football, competed in swimming, baseball, track & field, wrestled and especially the Martial Arts. The one thing I could not do was to speak out.

During those years, I excelled in sports, yet I was not able to be who I was really meant to be. In school, I knew that I knew the answers when the teacher asked questions of the class. My fear was that if I said something, even if it was correct that I was going to sound stupid. So, I didn't say a thing. Throughout most of my younger days in school I didn't speak up. When I got home, and my father would ask me questions and if it wasn't the right answer, I got beat up. And this just kept going and going and going. My stuttering got worse. In my selfworth got plunged.

And then a crazy thing happened. During the six grade and when I really wasn't thinking. I took a challenging test in which I ended getting the highest grade in the class. And that was flabbergasting to me. I started getting better and better grades. I started improving in many other areas of my life too.

Even in math, which didn't come easy to me earlier in my life, started flowing in like crazy. When I was in the seventh grade and I took algebra 1 and then in the eighth grade I took geometry. That progress continued all the way to calculus and beyond. The same thing happened in science. Junior high was a breakout time for me in a lot of different areas. While I still had the stuttering, I was able to open up and express myself in other ways. At that time, I was living in Savannah, GA and went to Beach Jr. High.

One of those was in singing. I entered a talent show with a couple of friends of mine. We did a James Brown number I remember. And we ended up winning the talent show. It really helped me to open up and other people saw me in a different light. Did you know that you can't stutter while singing?

Now while I was able to sing and do other things that came hard to me, the fear of speaking in public didn't go away. Even while in the Marines and later, in the LAPD I had plenty of "real" physical danger. Nothing brought forth the fear in me as being onstage and speaking in front of a group. I continued to stutter and that was a hinderance.

Being able to speak confidently in front of a group or any other public event was also something I always wanted to be able to do. And I didn't realize until years later why I had this tremendous fear. I didn't take a public speaking course or class because I also falsely believed that I would look stupid and that I would be judged. I believe that a lot of people fear that they would be judged and by exposing themselves speaking in public adds to it.

I went on a quest to learn how to make myself better by reading books, taking certain courses, and looking at the strategies of other people.

Mostly it became about going inside to find out why I had that fear and the reason why I do what I do. Even that still did not stop my fear of public speaking. Yet, I knew the only way to overcome that fear was to simply do it. In psychology we refer to this as exposure therapy.

One of my first actual speaking engagements, actually, not really a speaking engagement, but a presentation in front of a board. This was to present so that I can be on the board as well. I stood there facing these guys and looking at the eyes. My eyes started to glaze over my mouth started to get dry I swallowed him I was feeling nervous. I'd still like a deer in front of headlights. My stomach started shaking really bad and I felt like just passing out. And even throwing up.

There I stood, frozen, and started to talk. I was to present as to why I wanted to be on the board of this nonprofit organization. A friend has invited me to be a board member and I had to first, get through this interview/presentation. I told them that I wanted to make a difference. I was honest about my intentions.

And when I finished, and I had to wait about half an hour when they came out and told me that I was accepted onto the board. At that time, I didn't understand why they accepted me, since I was bad in speaking in public. Yet they told me I did pretty good. As I think back, I realized that we are our own worst critic. I know that I was my worst critic. It wasn't others judging me as I discovered. It was me judging myself. I learned that other people are always thinking about themselves and how people feel about them. That was a turning point when I discovered that truth.

I remember reading about taking small steps. This is been told through the years from different philosophers. It's been in fables, such as Aesops' "The Crow and the Pitcher" story. And much more. In Japan, the business philosophy of "Kaizen" mentions the power of small steps. Each small step leads to the greater goal.

Taking small steps towards overcoming fears and accomplishing goals is the key to success. And this is exactly what I did. I kept going at. With each small success my confidence in speaking in public grew as well as my competence. As I mentioned earlier about exposure therapy, it's is also based on taking small risks. Today I can happily say that what was once my greatest fear is now one of my greatest pleasures. From the platform of speaking on stage, I can address small or large crowds and thoroughly enjoy it. In front of those crowds I can express my message. I can help them to become the best versions of themselves. And this is exactly where I wanted to be right from my early years. That young boy that had no confidence in himself was able to overcome his greatest fear. I believe I've come full circle in terms of my journey. And that journey has led me to doing what I always wanted to do. And that was to truly help other people. That's what my mom would want to be to do. It's my calling.

Today, I can say that no matter what circumstances I face. What I'm doing as long as what I'm doing is to express my truth and my mission. That mission is focused towards helping others rise to their highest potential through self-actualization. I focus on surrounding myself with like-minded people, so we can all work together towards a common mission. I realize that that throughout my life, in whatever I did, I never did it alone. I had mentors, teachers, teammates, and so much more that helped me to reach a certain level and what I call success.

This story is not so much about me, but about my growing in those relationships that help me to transform. Without them, I could never be the person I've become. For me, they are the greatest. I want to thank each and every one of them. Without them, without my father doing what he did to me, without any challenge positive or negative I could never be where I'm at. It allowed me to face my fears and to grow by diving into them.

In this journey, I call my life, I realize it's not over. It simply continues all the way until the end. Until then, I have much more learning to do. More things to do. And more to give in the best way possible that I can give to help others.

On a side note, I retook the IQ test in 1985 and scored a 156.

And I just want to say to each person reading this. Find your journey. Find your mission. Find your truth. Face those fears and go at them head on. When you do, you're going to find the best version of yourself. Through your fears, you're going to be able to see the foundation of your highest potential. Simply go out there and do it. Do it often. Do it every day. Just do it.

By: Bob Choat

Representing: California

Who am I and Why am I Here? My Journey to Find Purpose & Relevance
By Adonia Dickson

For the most part, I was a relatively happy child. After all, my mom did everything she could to give my siblings and I a "normal" childhood. We were a close-knit family and enjoyed a variety of family activities together.

We played a lot of board games such as Scrabble, Monopoly, Backgammon, Twister, Connect Four, The Game of Life, Battleship, the list could go on and on. We would put large puzzles together at the kitchen table. It might take us a week or so to finish, but I looked forward to passing by the table for several minutes to see if I could put a few more pieces together.

My brother and I played jacks on the marble floor near the front door; it doesn't seem right, but he would always beat me. If I stop and think about it, he beat me at everything.

We went ice skating, and roller skated in San Francisco's Golden Gate Park. We would go camping and fishing. Yes, believe it or not, I fished too. I loved to fish, and I even put the worms on my hook. Getting the fish off the hook, well that's a different story.

Mom was "the cool mom," she always kept us busy and would take our friends and us to fun places like the movies, concerts, and plays. My sister on the other hand rarely hung out with us. She was often grumpy and acted annoyed all the time, especially when I was around. She spent most of her time with our Aunts.

I am the youngest of the three kids, and although I don't remember a lot about my younger years, I do remember my parents argued a lot. I guess it would be more accurate to say my dad did the arguing my mom, for the most part, would listen.

On one occasion I remember it was a cold and rainy night a few days before Easter. Mom was driving us to church to rehearse our Easter speeches.

As I reflect on it, I believe we were coming from shopping. We got new Easter clothes and new shoes. Mom was driving dad's brand-new shiny rust colored Cadillac. It was a sharp looking car, but what do I know, I was just a little girl about five or six years old at the time.

Suddenly, a speeding car came out of nowhere. The next thing I remember our car spun-out. We were spinning around and around, and before I knew it, we were looking at headlights then came BOOM, BANG, CRASH, we were tangled up in a pile of metal.

My head hit the dashboard, where my two front teeth planted themselves. Somehow my sister broke her jaw. I don't recall whether my mom had injuries, I think she may have hurt her back.

Nevertheless, there is no doubt her priority was on the wellbeing of my sister and me. But man-oh-man, I do remember seeing my dad stomping down the hospital corridor looking angry as ever. Perhaps I thought he was mad because someone caused an accident and hurt his "girls," but later I learned he was mad, more like "pissed off," because his new car was banged up. He was mad for weeks. I don't know where my brother was, he wasn't with us on this trip. I'm not sure if that was his choice, but my gut tells me my dad may have had something to do with it. My dad was clear and adamant that my brother wasn't going to be a "sissy," whatever that meant. I'm not sure I understood it at the time.

After the accident, mom and dad's relationship got worse. Dad seemed to always yell at mom, would leave the house or go to a separate room and mom would often cry. Then one day a "family meeting" was called.

My sister approached me saying mom wanted to tell us something. We all gathered in the living room, my brother, sister and me. Dad was noticeably missing.

My sister, the oldest, seemed to be angry all the time. She didn't enjoy hanging out with us; often she would go over to my grandmother's, or our aunt's house. She is a lot like my dad, bossy. She can be intimidating and sometimes outright mean. I never really knew why she carried herself that way, but many, many years later, well into our adulthood, we learned she was holding on to a deep dark secret. A secret that to this day I don't think is fully resolved.

My brother is 16 months older than me. He is a twin, but his twin died. If he were alive, I wonder what his name would be? I'm curious if he had lived, would he be like my brother. I truly love my brother so that would have been a good thing to have two loving brothers. But what if he had lived, would I have been born? Well, I was born, born into a life that for years was unfathomably lonely and dark, filled with struggle and pain because it didn't feel like I fit in.

Have you ever found yourself in such a dark place you just wanted to give up? You, often felt this deep, profound bottomless sadness that you would do almost anything to get rid of? That was me. To make things worse, I felt guilty for feeling this way. How dare I, what good reason did I have not to appreciate my life. I came from an average, fun loving family. We weren't perfect, but what family is?

How dare I! I had a roof over my head, heck I even had my own bedroom. There was food on the table, I did things and went places other kids would have loved to have gone. I was healthy, wasn't fighting a debilitating disease, poverty or abuse. I didn't have to struggle with a disability, nor exposure to a home filled with drugs or alcohol. How dare I feel that my life was awful and why did I have the audacity to feel sad and unhappy. What did I have to be sad and miserable about? My crime, I didn't like myself!

I was overly sensitive, insecure, required a lot of attention and needed constant reassurance that I was good enough. I would cry at the drop of a hat; especially if I thought someone was mean to me. I was often teased and felt every kid in the neighborhood would talk about me and call me names. What made me such an easy target?

I was an awkward and shy little girl. I don't know if I was particularly ugly, but I sure felt ugly. I guess one could say I went through an ungraceful growing period. The "ugly duckling" phase.

I went from having a round face, fat legs and my hair up in ponytails with cute little barrettes, to having a round head with a short coarse afro framing my face. I was often called "bald-headed" and other mean comments about my looks. I always felt I wasn't pretty, and there were many kids at school, boys, and girls who made sure to remind me every day! It should come to no surprise that I hated taking pictures. Seldom, if ever, did I take a picture I liked. To this day taking photos is a challenging experience for me.

The boys were just dumb boys joking around, but their teasing hurt me deeply. The girls were much crueler. They would get in my face, call me "bald-headed," then turn around and say to me, "you think you're pretty." This was so confusing, which one was I? Am I ugly and "bald-headed," or do I think I'm pretty? Surely, I couldn't be both.

I was often asked, "why are you so proper?" I guess it was a crime

for a little black girl to enunciate her words correctly. Was I wrong?

I couldn't seem to do anything right. But at least I was kind. I couldn't

be that bad, could I?

As I got older, my feelings of insecurity became worse, and I struggled with depression. I felt like a misfit and that everyone else was better and smarter than me.

Out of nowhere and completely unplanned, I became a teenage mom. In my late twenties, things got so dark and dismal; I couldn't see a way out. I was covered in doubt, hopelessness. and sadness. Life felt like a massive boulder was holding me down. I couldn't wait to go to bed, so that I couldn't feel anything. There were times where I didn't want to wake up.

One Saturday afternoon I made up my mind that I didn't want to live anymore. I decided I wanted to end my life. Thank god I couldn't even do that right. Thank god for reminding me that the little girl I had while I still managed to graduate from high school, needed me. Thank god for my role as a mom which became my reason to live at such a vulnerable time in my life.

The Turning Point

Think about a time in your life you found yourself wondering why you are here or what your purpose is? How was it possible that divine intervention took place, fertilized an egg which created this beautiful thing called "YOU." Think about it. You were that one specially selected that formed into one magnificent human being! That's a hell of a journey, an absolute miracle one might say.

If indeed we are the miracles that we are, why do so many of us feel we're not good enough. What story are you telling yourself? Who teased you, called you names, violated your trust, lied to you, cheated on you, stole from you, abused or disappointed you?

I have multiple stories of disappointment and let down, and I bet you do too. But just like a book with many chapters, you and I have the divine right and power to change our story and write a new chapter in this book called life.

> I was writing the same "Poor Me" chapter for many years! It's taken several do-overs, rewinds, ups, downs and turn around, but finally I sought help, read a lot, and prayed a lot. With the love of family and friends I began to see a glimmer of hope, possibility, potential, inspiration, anticipated and fought my way to a better life. It required me to change my "stinking thinking." How did I do it? By reading books. Books changed my thinking. Books saved my life! I learned that my life is extraordinary, and so is yours. You and I are one of a kind! A gift, what we have right now is the present. I'll leave you with three lessons I learned that ultimately saved my life.
>
> Lesson 1: Words Matter. Each and every word you say to yourself has everything to do with EVERYTHING you do! You are who you say you are, so choose your words wisely. Don't allow someone else's words define you or determine who you can become.
>
> Lesson 2: Hope changes lives. This quote says it best, "If it's to be, it's up to me." - Author unknown. Each of us is like a blank canvas; we create each brush stroke that determines our masterpiece.
>
> Lesson 3: Adversity, difficulty, and hardship will come "Difficulties come not to obstruct but to instruct."
>
> Below are more of my favorite quotes that became part of my journey to a purposeful life:

If you are not willing to risk, you can't grow, and if you can't grow you cannot become your best, and if you cannot become your best, you can't be happy and if you can't be happy, what else is there?" — Les Brown

"If you let bad things stop you, you won't be here for the good things." — Unknown

"Solving a problem takes a different mind than the one that created it." — Albert Einstein

"Success is a few simple disciplines practiced every day." — Jim Rhon

"Man can live about forty days without food, about three days without water, about eight minutes without air… but only one second without hope." — Hal Lindsey

"Good, better, best. Never let it rest. 'Till your good is better and your better is best – St. Jerome

"No one can make you feel inferior without your consent" — Eleanor Roosevelt

"Giving up on your goal because of one setback is like slashing your other three tires because you got a flat." — Unknown

"Try to be a rainbow in somebody cloud" – Maya Angelo

"If you think you are beaten, you are

If you think you dare not, you don't

If you like to win but think you can't, it is almost certain you won't

If you think you'll lose, your lost

For out of the world we find,

Success begins with a fellow's will

It's all in the state of mind.

If you think you are outclassed, you are

You've got to think high to rise,

You've got to be sure of yourself before you can ever win a prize.

Life's battles don't always go to the stronger or faster man,

But soon or late the man who wins is the man who thinks he can." — Think and Grow Rich; Napoleon Hill

"If God brings you to it, he will bring you through it.

Happy moments, praise God   Difficult moments, seek God

    Quiet moments, worship God   Painful moments, trust God

    Every moment, Thank God."

Excerpt from Being Spiritual - Connecting with God and Ourselves by Paul E. Jones

My wish is one of these quotes inspires you and leads you to a life fulfilled with Peace & Blessings

Business Name: Awe-Inspiring Leadership Group
Business e-mail: adonia@awe-inspiringleadership.com

Representing: Uganda

HOPE FOR NASENYI FOUNDATION David Daka

My Name is David Kenneth Daka, a husband to my beautiful wife Cathy, and a father to our two amazing Children, Taavi 12-year girl and Toviel 10-year-old boy, I am the founder and President of Hope For Nasenyi Foundation, a nonprofit that is promoting Education for orphans and less privileged children and addressing women/mothers' basic needs in Nasenyi, one of the communities in Eastern Uganda, Africa.

In 1995, while still a small and young boy, I lost my parents. My father was buried on July 1st, and my mother on September 18th of the same year. I was the 9th child to my mother, and to my Dad, I cannot exactly tell. This is a fact. My father was a polygamous Dad. My parents both died of HIV-AIDS. As a small boy in such a big family, I was not exposed to so much knowledge of either the disease or what they actually died of. It was after some time that I made sense of several events. Now being an orphan is not a very unique occurrence, but to me, being of a tender age, and losing my parents within a span of two and half months apart, and especially losing my mother who was a very close friend and partner to me was unique.

As a son growing up, and growing up as a last born, I was so close to my mother, and her only living child then that lived with her least of time, my mother provided for all my needs. For her to die at such a time, and of course losing both parents at such a time, I lost hope in my life. I had no idea what my tomorrow could bring. As a matter of fact, I lost everything. As an individual, I lost everything. Tears were my food for a long period.

As a family, we lost, as a home, we lost everything too. Our relatives that should and could have been very supportive at such a time took all the property that we had as a family. There is no moment I had ever experienced in my life such as this in 1995. Our parents were defined as a middle-income family, so we grew up in a financially well-built family and home. But in Uganda, we do not have a strong insurance policy to take care of such times, the reason our relatives left us with completely nothing. So, we were barely left with nothing. To illustrate that we actually lost everything including money, I could not even afford transport money back to school. In my society, when someone dies, friends and relatives offer money to support the family with all the funeral arrangements. One of my late brothers who was called Emmy was able to pick some money from such offerings for me to go to school. So, this probably meant that we needed more family members to pass in order to have some money brought to us. Such events were so sad and brought more misery to me as a young boy and losing even the little hope that I could have.

Life happened so quickly that the community redefined us. The poor people in the community, and those that we knew were poor referred to us as poor. Now have you ever referred to as poor by a poor person? If a poor person referred to you as poor, then you must be really poor. With this kind of background, losing my parents within a span of two and half months in the same year, losing them to HIVAIDS, being left with totally nothing in life, waking up to days that I had no idea if I would grab something to eat, walking down the streets with nowhere to go, being referred to as poor by the poor in Africa was such a life shuttering experience that I lost hope.

This background over the years got me involved to relate to innocent children that live a life that I could relate to. This is how I birthed the idea of founding a nonprofit foundation.

Representing: Vietnam

YOU CAN'T WIN BEING AVERAGE

They say that the average person is always at his best, his place of comfort is always his place of rest. He will never strive for anything more or anything less. My story is simple. I struggle with a common disease that most people never learn to deal with. It's called living a life of mediocrity or being average. – Tuan Nguyen

On March 14, 2014, I was arrested with over 400 grams of methamphetamines. I remember sitting in the back of the police car completely speechless. I knew at that moment in my life that God's call on me was great. When I got to county and I was facing 35 years for being a repeat offender. Through the grace and mercy of God, the judge granted me 16 years.

The beginning of my incarceration was all about learning how to adjust. It wasn't hard for me because I had been in prison before. For most of us, it's part of a vicious cycle. I've watched countless men get released from prison only to come back a few years later. This became one of my greatest fears because I never wanted to

> come back to prison, but that's exactly what happen to me. I realized that as a child of God, we will always receive correction from God. Our paths are different from those of the world. We will suffer and encounter much affliction in our lives for the glory of God.

The question I pose is: What makes so many offenders come back to prison? It definitely wasn't the food and the bunk beds! I used to think it was the power of addiction upon our lives but one day God spoke to me and said, Tuan, you don't have a drug problem! You have a self-image problem! You still don't know who you are in Christ! He was absolutely right. I spent my whole life adopting borrowed beliefs. I was a natural people pleaser and an affirmation junkie. I found comfort in the affirmation and acceptance of other people. Here's the problem with that: I was seeking to find purpose and identity from people that didn't know who they were as well. It was like the blind leading the blind. I found myself living a life of performance. Always striving to meet the expectations of others. I was the epitome of the Yes Man!

They say that you can never outperform your self-image. Whatever a person thinks of themselves will always manifest no matter what they say. We can never perform consistently in a way we truly don't believe. Therefore, we cannot travel into the next stage of growth and development until we first travel within. I realized that borrowed beliefs could only take me so far. I would have to believe in myself even when others didn't. Due to many mistakes and failures in my life, I found refuge in living in my fear of failure. Afterall, it was easier that way. You can't fail if you don't try. At least that was my philosophy at that time. Places of comfort became my way of life and since I was a pretty good communicator, I would convince myself that it was good. I became content with just being average, living life simply by default.

Something I would hear a lot growing up and throughout prison was, "Tuan, you have so much potential!" Let me remind you that to an average person seeking to find purpose, this sounds very exciting! So, I began believing that I had potential, but I had no idea in what. I believed that one day someone would discover my potential and give me the opportunity of a lifetime. Let's just say this, hope and pretending is not a strategy in growth and development. You must tap into your potential. One of my favorite phrase's states; your discovery zone begins when your comfort zone ends.

Someone once asked me: how do you get comfortable being uncomfortable? The answer, I AM ENOUGH! Through incarceration, God was developing me into becoming a leader. Like the story of Joseph, God had to deliver me from the things of this world in order to develop me into my destiny. I remember listening to John Maxwell one day in leadership class when he posed the question, "What is your dream and who is on your team?" At that moment, I realized that I never really had a dream. This caused me to really evaluate my life and identify where I was going and who was coming with me. God showed me that not everyone could come with me on this journey, so quit trying to take everyone with me. It was in moments like this, where God would use John Maxwell to speak into my life and mentor me through books and videos. Through studying the laws of growth, I decided one night that I would go all in and tap into my potential and find my purpose. I began chasing my passion and that was in becoming a motivational speaker! I began investing in myself as a leader, coach and trainer using the principles of John Maxwell. I knew that the only way I could help people was by making myself more valuable. You can only add value to others when you first value yourself. I started seeing a vision of transforming prison culture through leadership training and communication. God showed me a vision of joining the John Maxwell Team, so I could come back to Prison Fellowship and reproduce leaders. In late October of 2018, I stepped out in faith and joined the greatest leadership team in the world, the John Maxwell Team. My vision is for the transformation of men and women in prison through the teachings of John Maxwell. Today I am linked up with brothers and sisters that are all over the globe that serve a mighty God. I stand today as a living testimony of what God can do through Prison Fellowship and John Maxwell. I found my niche while in prison and today average is no longer good enough. You can't win in life being average, so therefore be the best you can be.

Representing: New York

Pushed into My Destiny Yolanda Ayo

2017 was the year I decided to try something new. These past years have taken me on quite a ride. It hasn't been easy, but it has certainly been worth it. This journey has taught me that life is like a roller coaster–there are ups, downs, twists, and turns but eventually you'll begin to coast.

In 2000, I graduated from college and like most graduates I was aggressively searching for that next step. I began pounding the pavement looking for a job. I went to job fair after job fair, interview after interview and after a few months, I landed my first job with an insurance company. Yay! My time has finally come, or so I thought. I had gone thru the on boarding process and was slated to start that summer. Well, two weeks before my start date, I get a phone call from the Human Resources Manager, He said, "Yolanda, I'm so sorry we did not have the green light to hire you. I'm so sorry." I was crushed.

After shedding a few tears, I took a deep breath and contacted my former college professor. He gave me the contact number for a recruitment firm in Westchester and the rest is history. I began my career in the healthcare recruitment industry. In a nutshell, my job was placing healthcare professionals in mid to senior level positions serving some of the top healthcare organizations in the New York TriState area. It was a role that I enjoyed for many years and was successful in.

Even though things were going well, as the years went by, I began to feel stagnant. There were many instances where I wanted to leave but fear reared its ugly head. I'd sit in my office looking out the window thinking about life, asking myself, "What is next for me?" I've always thought about entering the retail/fashion industry, especially once I had my children, but I was afraid of taking my family on a ride of uncertainty. Plus, I was in a secure role with allot of flexibility and when you are a parent it is those flexibilities that become of more value. Had I thought about it even deeper, I would have realized that this thing called life is filled with uncertainty. It's all trial and error.

Fast forward to 2017. After nearly 17 years of service, the doors of the medical search firm that I was devoted too closed and I was left feeling broken. I was broken because I felt like a failed myself. I allowed fear to guide my steps to the point where I couldn't make a step. The 'secure' job that I held on too for so many years left me and there was nothing I could do about it; no turning back. As I drove out of the parking garage one last time, I took a deep breath, wiped those tears and said a silent prayer. I said, "Lord, I don't know what the future holds but I do know that you hold my future…."

The thought of entrepreneurship kept dancing in my mind. This was my time, my moment to start exploring. Unique Finds for Kids was an idea I had written down years ago in one of my spiral notebooks at work. I figured it will be a place where parents and grandparents can find quality, sustainably-made, everyday wear and specialty pieces for that special someone in their lives. Without any business or retail experience I felt uncertain (there goes that word again).

I began taking business classes and attending networking events while keeping an open mind throughout my journey. I had an eagerness to learn, connect, and build. It was that same feeling I felt fresh out of college. It was important for me to not only spread my wings but to also lift off and fly.

It is with a thankful heart that I'm happy to finally say that I am a business woman. Unique Finds for Kids is here! The road ahead is long but there is beauty in hustling for myself and for my family. I'm finally doing something that I've never done before, I'm feeding my soul; allowing myself to be free. The blessing is that with every purchase made on my website, a portion of the proceeds will be donated to the Parkinson's Foundation to raise awareness and continued research towards a cure. This is an illness that hits close to home as my father and brother are currently battling this illness.

I must admit what I thought was going to be a tiny side gig has quickly become a much larger entity than even I could imagine. It is obvious that God has bigger plans for me. It's scary! I have had moments of great emotion but to God be the glory I'm here. Most importantly, my children get to see the "Mompreneur" in me. When I was in my previous role, my kids watched as I'd head out to work every single day, but they didn't know exactly what I did for a living. Now my children have a front row seat to this entire process. It's a family affair! It's amazing what will happen when you build the courage to pursue your dreams. It warms my heart to hear my daughter, Morgan say with joy, "My Mom has her own business." She wears my brand with pride. She is right by my side as a Buyer at local trade show events. She is absorbing it all. She tells me all the time, "Mommy, you are Magic." My son Avry says, "Mommy, I'm proud of you." My eyes well up with tears when my husband says, "You can do it!" My regret is that I didn't begin this entrepreneurial process sooner.

To the individuals who are contemplating entrepreneurship, go for it! We have one life to live, so live it! Align yourself with likeminded individuals who you can lean on during this roller-coaster ride. My support and inspiration come from family, friends, fellow business owners, and my mentor at Shanbhag Enterprises. Trust me! Don't let fear hinder you from your dreams. It's never too late to explore new interests. We are entitled to changing the narrative. Once you open yourself up to the idea of change, opportunities will present themselves and connections will be made that will be beneficial to your growth as an entrepreneur.

> Entrepreneurship is not for the faint of heart. Influencer Cheryl Woods says it best, "Walk into every room knowing that you belong, stop declining your seat at the table because you feel inadequate or unqualified. The more you take a seat at the table, the more qualified you become." It's going to take time, hard work and dedication, lots of research, patience, and development. It's going to require wearing many, many hats. Wear them! Juggle them! Work it!

Don't be afraid to embark on a journey of your own. As for me, my journey continues.....

- Yolanda

Founder/CEO Company: www.UniqueFindsForKids.com

Representing: Jordan

Endings and Beginnings by Sofie Nubani

The most profound moment of my life is when I had a true soul wakeup call. It was one that felt very hurtful and very disappointing at that time. It almost made me feel like my past life was like being lived part of a movie scene until that moment, only to see all the characters changing roles. This was from close family members to friends. I felt like it was another world one that was not familiar and cold.

After my mom passed away a lot of changes in my personal family dynamics also changed. Never under estimate a strong mother, women and wife role in a household. For the first time ever I truly felt alone, this time it was after the end of my just over two years marriage.

> Was the world just changing to a very unfamiliar way or was it just my new reality? I come from a very family-oriented culture and background but what I was experiencing was a lot of separation and distance, not in miles or locations, but in hearts and communications. It was my new reality.

I must say it was hard to observe. The closest description of how I felt was experiencing the emotion of abandonment and wow!!! I just truly realized the true feeling I was living as I am writing about my story. I must share the only thing that truly helped me go through my deep-felt pain and all these changes was my faith, myself love, my self-respect and honor, my refusing to ABANDON me. I learned how to be there for myself and I mean be my best cheerleader, my best friend, my best encourager, my best comforter. You see in life one thing is constant and that is change, that's why we must be flexible enough to deal with it as it arrives opposite from what we had planned or wished for.

When I got married for the second time after many years of being single my goal and intention was not to be divorced. With, a big lesson in life I learned that by staying focused on the direction and not the goal, helps one adapt to and course correct better and faster, when things go contrary to one's plan.

It was a period of two weeks that truly allowed me to understand many new emotions that were visiting me. They were not pleasant, but they became my best teachers. It is much easier writing about them today than living them by the minute. Let me tell you going through disappointments as a child while I still had my family, a roof over my head, siblings to talk to and interact with, parents that provided all our basic needs and more is a lot easier than going through shocks, disappointments and more as an adult and your whole life and family dynamic changes. I had my moments of insecurities, doubts and uncertainties. They all surrounded me within that time frame, but I just could not live with that suffering. It was longer than needed. I recognized I must make a choice.

Do I want to be a victim of my circumstance or a victor over them?

Do I want to spend the rest of my life feeling sorry for things I have no control of or do I want to create a healthier environment for myself? Do I want to be a slave to my mind or do I want it to be my servant?

You see to make everything go away and instantly live the life I was accustomed to; all I had to do was obey my family's request. That is to go back and live in Jordan, have my dad's full support A to Z. I do come from a culture that a man always is the provider to his wife or daughter when needed. That would have been the easiest thing to do.

However, it conflicted with my emotional core value of freedom, that I later learned about myself after studying for my Neurolinguistic Programming (NLP) certification program. I do recommend NLP for anyone reading this to know your emotional core values, your pain values and your gain values as they will help you go through life with more clarity and understanding.

Freedom was something that I valued and could never compromise. When you honor your truth, speak your truth and live your truth you will feel free and live with inner peace. As I reflected on my life going through all these changes, I realized that all past choices I made including ones that caused me to suffer were made in honor to my soul's freedom. In the beginning it is always challenging, know that in the long term it will pay off! At least you can say you wrote the manuscript of the story of your life in your own words. I loved my family but couldn't live my life to passed down traditions and culture rules from many generations to locations and reality of thousands of years ago. I honor a lot in my culture and many others; however, I have learned through my own experience and spiritual journey truths that have directed me to the wisdom of my own soul. My higher consciousness and inner compass have made me more mindful and aware to how I live my life and what is important in my journey.

I learned that all the sleepless nights were my own cosmic alarm clock. My soul awaking, my true discovery to one of the most important lows of the universe: the law of detachment.

I learned that a lot of my answers were all explained just from the process of birth and death.

I learned about my connection to the word freedom. I mean when I just hear that word my whole soul lightens up. I breathe better and feel lighter.

So, one day as I was driving to the beach feeling a little heavy, took my notepad and a pen and not realizing that was the day I learned a lot about myself. I remember asking myself what does the word freedom means to me, why it grabbed me, why am I so connected to it, and how I can always live feeling free as a spirit, as a soul?

What came to me was: When we are born the umbilical cord is cut immediately after birth. A mother is a supporter, yet we were not meant to remain attached. When we die, we die alone and that no one, not even out parents, spouse, children or siblings accompanies us in our graves. That by the law of nature, creation and the universe we are meant to be free as we are born, and it is how we leave. I learned that there is much wisdom to be extracted from that. Then I asked, how could one achieve the true meaning of freedom?

What came to me are the "CHOICES" we make in our life lead us to where we end up. Then I asked how could I make choices that will make me feel free? The answer that I received was that 1st, one had to be "CONVINCED" on "WHY" we are making these choices and then 2nd, convinced in the choices made. Then I asked, if I believe in my choices and are convinced about them then why I had to still suffer when I did. The answer that came to me then was "COURAGE"! You must have courage to take action.

> WOW! I not only knew I had this special connection to the word "freedom", but I now understood how to achieve it in my life as it was broken down to me in moments of contemplation and stillness just channeling divine energy and connecting with cosmic forces. I highly recommend making time to connect and center away from all the background noise and distractions of one's life. I remember driving back from the beach that day feeling so light as if someone carried me all the way back home.

I learned with my experience how to transform the feeling of loneliness to creative adventure. Learning new things has always helped me to get my focus on things that are inspiring and supportive to my journey instead of focusing on what is not working. Signing for a new class, traveling to a new country or discovering a new city, reading a new book, creating new projects all made me comfortable with my aloneness.

I understood later why I was meant to be so alone and disconnected from everything including people that I was so connected with. It was in this period of my life when I discovered my true powers. Growing up as a child I was known to be extremely sensitive. I remember in high school my teacher yelled at me for talking in class and I had tears silently rolling on my face. I had worked on myself quite a bit through the years.

I went to seminars, workshops, and events all to help myself learn and grow to the next level. When I couldn't afford to go, I would listen to YouTube videos of all the people that were inspiring to me. That always helped expand my mind, also helped me see things from a different prospective. I encourage you to do the same. If you're going through a rough time don't stay in a corner self-sabotaging, blaming or feel guilty about what's going on. Instead, train your mind to think of solutions and remind yourself of the potential to unlimited possibilities that are waiting for you.

I learned to stay on a higher level of thinking. In this period I evolved so much and faster than I ever can recall. You see all the times I invested in myself paid off in good dividends. I learned a lot. I got certified as Laughter Yoga™ Instructor, EFT & TFT Practitioner, Reiki Master Teacher, Cheos Master Teacher, Social and Emotional Intelligence Coach, Motivational Speaker, Life Coach and more. I share this with you to let you know that every step I took to help myself, truly served me well.

You see if you want to maintain a beautiful outdoors to your home, you will need to pay attention to your landscaping, possibly your pool and so forth. To keep your grass nice and trim you will need the right tools to keep it up. If you want your pool to look good and stay clean you need the right tools to do that. Without the proper equipment and materials that won't be possible. Just like if someone has heart attack and needs an immediate open-heart surgery, just knowing the right doctor or going to the best hospital is not going to be enough. They also need the right tools for the surgeon to work with. It's the same thing in life; you need the right tools that you can tap into and use, depending on the issues you're facing or circumstances you're dealing with.

You are your best investment and the best gift you can share with your loved ones and humanity, is living the best version of you.

I signed up for my Laughter Yoga™ certification while spending last days in the hospital with my mother who was fighting stage four colon cancer for the past year and a half and was given ten more days to live from that time. (This took place in Amman, Jordan, which is the capital and my country of origin.) I knew I would need a major distraction after leaving to go back to US. I had an exceptional mother and it was not going to be easy to deal with her loss. It was the biggest loss our family faced and truly is irreplaceable. However, I was thankful until this day that I took that course as it has helped me a lot on many different levels.

I had just opened a company a year before my divorce and offered services in all the things I learned. It was fulfilling. It felt like a paid hobby as it was doing what I loved most. My company's name was Transcendence and I started it from home. I kept my first job selling vacation ownership (which I have done for many years). It was enjoyable. I helped families invest in insuring future vacations with their loved ones, investing in their health and make their dream vacations a living reality, yet being able to leave a legacy behind as they can pass their vacation ownership down.

I have a grown, handsome, and smart independent son who I am so proud of and blessed to have, Rawy Rayan who I pray for success, peace, wisdom and good health over his life. He is a young man who is focused with great leadership skills, was not my young child anymore. He had his life and purpose to fulfill. Having a child is a beautiful gift, yet, I learned our children are not our own as they are also meant to be free. Again, understanding more the depth of the law of detachment is not easy one, but one that allows you to truly evolve and practice unconditional love.

Being single has allowed me to get busy with projects I enjoyed and also the freedom I needed to truly be clear on my purpose. It allowed me to connect with my heavenly gifts, to be able to see them and open them. I love uplifting, encouraging, empowering, relaxing and making people laugh. I love to remind people to walk into their own magnificence, to claim their own power and not to let anything or anyone dull their sparkle. I love to remind people to let their smile change the world not the world change their smile.

Being in service is a passion to my heart. It is what allowed me to heal, grow and evolve. I was able to build such a great relationship with myself. Emotional Mastery is an everyday practice for me. I learned that happiness was not a destination but a daily practice, choosing one positive thought over negative one that is not supportive to my journey. I had outgrown some relationships and eliminated some toxic ones. I learned to be true to what supports my highest good and to be more selective in whom I allow in my inner circle.

> I learned that being in service is my soul calling as I always heard that inner voice saying: I am servant of light (that I shall honor). However, whom I surround myself with on daily basis are those who I feel are authentic and possess qualities that resonate and are aligned with my soul: those with a growth mindset and are seeking to do better, to learn more and to grow. Meaning, these people don't grow older, they grow up with time. When they say: "You are who you surround yourself with" there is much truth to it. Be very mindful of who you receive and share energy from and to. Raise your standards and do not settle for anything less than what you are deserving of.
> You can never replace time that you lost or buy inner peace. It is

your everyday choices only that can support to maximize and optimize living the best version of you. Choose wisely!

My personal challenges including cultural differences and religious beliefs, which all helped me expand my vision and understand things beyond just the physical. I meditated often and always connected with light energy for so many years.

I remember doing guided meditations to my sister in law and neighbor years before I even knew what the word guided mediation meant. I would have them both lay on the sofas in my living room, put on soft music and ask them to imagine themselves in a place of nature and so on. One day while I was at the local Barnes & Noble bookstore looking to pick some self-help audios to listen to as I drive. I saw one audio about Guided meditation for beginners. I picked it up. While it said it was not recommended to listen to it while driving, I remained parked and started listing to it. OMG, I thought to myself it was so similar to what I was doing and never had known it is actually a practice. I had just recently moved to the states and English was not my first language, I did not even hear or know before what the word meditation meant.

I had signed up for a Cheos Energy Healing class and advanced fast in it and become a Certified Cheos Master Teacher as I have been connecting with light energy for many years prior. I used light energy in my meditations and daily life for many different things. I come to know there are actually many meditation modalities including Reiki, which I as well studied and become a Certified Reiki Master. All of them, including my Crystal Healing certification and more, also included light energy as a method of channeling, charging and connecting with Cosmic Intelligence and divine light. I loved expanding my awareness to matters and subjects that introduced themselves prior to me. It felt like I have lived in that light's energy many past lives. It all felt comfortable, known and familiar to my soul. Connecting with myself has become more fun.

The more I connected the more aware and clear I felt. Love this quote by Socrates:

"Know thyself" as this was great advice and deep wisdom to follow. I had spent many days alone and learned more and more about my life and myself. I had experienced the joy of soul searching and going to deeper and higher realms. It was clear to me that we experience sadness, depression, stress and more, when we stop learning, when we stop creating, when we stop growing.

Laughter Mindset™ Program

I had signed up in late 2017 for peak performance coaching with Bob Choat. He took me through many growth challenges in order help me to transform. I met Bob through Facebook and Googled him to find out more information. There was quite a bit and I was looking forward to learning more about him and his services. We talked back and forth. During this time, I went to Tennessee (due to Hurricane Irma heading towards Florida) and Bob was dealing with fires in California. We reconnected to start the coaching sessions.

During one coaching session between me (coachee) and Bob Choat (coach) we discussed the power of laughter. I mentioned that I was a Laughter Yoga™ Instructor and Bob Choat stated that he was a Laughter Facilitator. I was surprised and started to laugh. So, did Bob. Well, that laughing went for over an hour. It turns out that we caught the laughter virus. We laughed so hard that trying to stop only kept it going harder. I was trying to stop it by saying: OUR MINDSET we needed a change of mindset to help us stop.

Bob's mind swirled a bit and he had an "aha" moment. He blurted out LAUGHTER MINDSET! He then doodled a child character laughing and wrote down The Laughter Mindset Program.

From there the Laughter Mindset Program ™ was born. Since then, we created the outline to the program and incorporated modalities and teachings from areas such as psychology, neuroscience, Neurolinguistic Programming (NLP), TFT and EFT Tapping,

meditation, hypnosis, fitness, the science of laughter and more...
The Laughter Mindset™ Program does truly incorporate many areas that enhance the whole program.

Through weeks of discussions on how to best present this program, we decided on doing workshops. That way we could both test the concepts in the initial workshops and develop it further.

At every workshop we received great feedback. The first workshop was conducted at the University of Central Florida (UCF) Barbara Ying Center on May 18, 2018. True to form of finding humor in everyday life, the GPS took us to the wrong location, we had to call around to find the Barbara Ying Center. Arriving late to our own workshop, myself I (and Bob) was able to take control by telling the participants that the tables needed to be moved out and the chairs arranged in a semi-circle.

We had a great turnout. I thought I did well, especially since this was the first time, I conducted a workshop and with no facilitating training.

> Bob threw me to the wolves and I thrived. Each subsequent workshop, I was able to facilitate with no practice beforehand. This shows one that it is important to have the knowledge of the subjects being taught and the passion to teaching.
>
> The next workshop was conducted at The IV Lounge at Dr. Philips in Orlando. Like the last one, we barely went over the program other than having the outline of what was going to be taught and going over those areas. We did well again. We partially introduced Laughter Fitness to the mix, another segment of the Laughter Mindset Program that we are excited about.
>
> On August 26, 2018, we brought the Laughter Mindset™ Program to the Sheraton Resorts recently merged with (Marriott) today is known to be one of the top 100 Fortune companies located in n Orlando Florida. During the workshop, we fully introduced Laughter Fitness to the program. Two different exercises were done. The feedback

again was great. In this workshop, I thought I did my best facilitating of any one so far.

In the three workshops done during this time period, there was much growing that was done and discussions going back and forth. While the birthing period was necessary, we realized that to take the program to the next level was a necessity. We pondered as to what to do.

Before the 3rd workshop at the Sheraton and during a whole week of discussions, we went back and forth to what was needed. What we came come up with was a 12-week program where each person would be able to take his or her mindset to a higher level, a "meta" level. Hence, The M.E.T.A. Shift Program was born.

The M.E.T.A. Shift Program is an advanced high-level coaching program designed to take a person from where he or she is at and into a beyond transformed to a fully actualized self.

More programs and retreats are planned for the future. The Laughter Mindset™ Program is now being described as The Laughter Mindset™ Experience. The reason for this is that it's all about the experience one will get that will help each participant to transform. Laughter helps to facilitate that transformation. The foundation of what the program is all about will always be there, even when improvements are made.

Laughter and a Growth Mindset are the foundations. When we are open to learning new things and let go of one's personal biases, a growth mindset happens. What is taught is that to be more aware of one's personal biases will help to squash those same biases and go from a closed mind to a more open one.

We will list the Laughter Mindset™ Experience at our website:

laughtermindset.com

where one can learn more about it and invest into the program. For those that want to grow to their highest and best self, The M.E.T.A. Shift Program will also be listed.

In the About Me page, both Dr. Bob Choat and myself Sofie Nubanil will have our short biographies and our contact information.

Remember: YOU DON'T STOP LAUGHING BEACOUSE YOU GROW OLD. YOU GROW OLD BECAUSE YOU STOP LAUGHING.

At Laughter Mindset, a place you don't just visit, you'll shift state right away. Now, breathe and laugh… HA HA HA!

M :
Mindset
Mission
Meaning

E :
Evolve

T :
Transformation

A:
Actualization

M.E.T.A SHIFT

http://laughtermindset.com/meta-shift/

Representing: The United Kingdom

Step into Your Greatness Dr. Patrick Businge

I was not born in the greatness of Great Britain but in the poverty of Uganda. Although, I lived there during the war, I did not let war live in me. I remember that on one night when we had just finished our dinner, we were preparing to sleep. Suddenly, there were noises and gunshots outside. Running out for safety, my family and I ran into the banana plantations and spent the night there. When we came back in the morning, a large part of our house was destroyed, my parent's shop had been burgled, and my primary school had been turned into an army barracks. I remember having to travel in a refugee truck to a new village where our lives resumed but was never the same again.

Under these circumstances, I could never have ever imagined that I would study in 7 Universities and gain over 7 university qualifications. I could have never imagined that I would go on to create my own university and help people step into their greatness. So, what made the difference? It's really very simple, education. Education was my passport to a winning world.

I did not let my circumstances derail my dreams for a better future. I always maintained that war wasn't a permanent condition. I rose above my circumstances and made greatness my benchmark. So, I let my belief drive my conviction in education. Education helped me realize that though I lived in war, I should not let war live in me. Education helped me to understand that though I lived in poverty, I should not let poverty live in me. Education helped me realize that both poverty and war were not permanent. I did not let war kill my dream of studying in a world class university like Cambridge. It fueled me to walk many miles to school barefoot and work in plantations under the heat of the sun to raise money for my school fees. My dream was finally realized when I completed my PhD from Exeter University, one of the finest universities in the world.

I am now an educator and have taught over 50,000 people in classrooms, churches, orphanages, villages, community centers, and boardrooms throughout the United Kingdom, Europe, Africa, and the Americas. I am a strong believer in lifelong learning and personal development. Living in a world characterized by war, plagued by a shortage of hope and marred

with average performance, my ultimate vision is to inspire one million people to become instruments of peace, messengers of hope and channels of greatness. I do this through the university I created, Greatness University: world's first institution dedicated to discovering, unlocking, and monetizing greatness in individuals and businesses.

Through my work at Greatness University, I help people escape physical, mental and moral poverty through education. At Greatness

University, we believe that greatness leaves clues. We are therefore committed to helping people like you tap into their greatness faster and easily than you can ever imagine. We do this by researching what makes people great, organizations flourish, and businesses thrive. We find out what drives people to become great in all spheres of life. We help people create their personal economies by monetizing their greatness. We guide people on the best ways to create lasting legacies. We work daily and tirelessly so that the people we love are also left with lasting legacies of greatness that we hope will live on long after they are gone.

The civil rights activist, singer and author Maya Angelou says, 'There is no greater agony than bearing an untold story inside you'. I believe you have an untold story within you. Your story does not need to go unheard. Your story needs to be written and spoken so that whoever reads or listens to it can say, 'It is because of you, I did not give up on life'.

In effect, I help people discover, develop and deliver their stories. As a Book Creation Coach, my team and I run retreats on how to discover, write, publish and monetize books. I myself have authored 7 published works and it gives me immense pleasure to know that they have been well received by the public and other authors as well. It gives me immense satisfaction that these books are helping me achieve my goal of creating enough other greatness leaders who will carry the legacy forward.

I not only help people write their stories, but I also give them the opportunity to co-author with me and share their stories on Greatness TV where I host the new and popular show You Changed My Life. In less than 3 months, I have hosted over 20 guests and co-authors. Again, it gives me immense satisfaction that through the examples of others, I can encourage others to do the kind of work that motivates and inspires them to create their best lives. There is greatness in you. I look forwards to helping you discover your greatness and create your best life.

Representing: Florida

Don't Get Held Hostage to A Job!

I was held hostage to a job. I had a job that paid a very good salary with unlimited overtime. At the time, I had a young son around seven years old and my husband was in the Navy and sailing around the world most of the time. My job was everything to me and too many of the employees that work there. The money was flowing, and I could travel. I was given an American Express Corporate card and many other perks. When I say the money was flowing, I am talking about really flowing. But I was working so much, I really didn't have time to spend it. I didn't have time for anything. I didn't have time for my son, church, family or friends. I put my faith in my career instead of my Heavenly Father. All I lived and breathe was this job. Whenever they requested me to do something, I did it. I always wanted to be the top performer. The most liked employee and the employee with the most overtime. They were given out so many awards and I had to win every single one of them. I even won the employee with the most overtime. I was averaging close to seventy-five hours of overtime a pay period. Whenever they needed someone to travel on a moment notice, I would volunteer. I wouldn't think twice about making arrangements for someone to watch my son. The next-door neighbor was very nice to me and my son and didn't mind looking after him when he got home from school. He came home to an empty house many days. The grace of God and his mercy watched over my son. Just thinking about how negligent I was as a mother saddens me to this day. But I was hostage to that job by choice. Greed and having the big paycheck every two weeks were my own selfish choice. I would take some money out of my paycheck and put it in a safe that I kept under the bed. I remember after a few months I had accumulated over sixteen thousand dollars in cash. I remember working while I was sick. My heart was constantly racing. I started to lose weight. I didn't care. I wouldn't take off to go to the doctor. I was cold all the time and eating ice all day. But I didn't care. I wanted to have the most overtime and a big fat paycheck. I wanted the recognition as the most loyal and dependable employee ever. But I thank God for his deliverance. I've never done drugs in my whole entire life. But I was addicted to this company and money. Some

people don't understand that when you sacrifice everything for something and that's all you want to do, it is an addiction. However, God had other plans for me. One day, the big Whigs from corporate came down to visit our office and we thought that it was just to see how well the Jacksonville, Florida office was doing. We put on the Ritz for them. Some of the ladies including myself did a dance routine like we were some kind of NFL cheerleaders. I can laugh about it now. But then the company's president got up and made an announcement that change our lives. He said very matter of fact "We have made a decision to relocate all of our offices to one central location in Arizona". They were not giving us an option to transfer but will give all of us a severance package. We will also have to train the employees in Arizona. The room was quiet in disbelief for a moment. Then you heard sobbing. I remember our local Vice President turning beet red. I was numb. I am thinking maybe I misunderstood. I know this couldn't be happening. But yes it was. I had sacrificed everything for this company. Ten years of money, money, money. What will I do now? I had basically forgot how to be social. I didn't know how to be a mom. I felt like I was on an island by myself. They stopped the overtime immediately. They offered us interviewing and resume classes. Now, I had time to realize how sick I was. You see my legs were swelling up daily to a point that I could barely walk. But when I was working so much, I kept myself busy and blocked out the fact that my legs were swollen every day. I fainted a couple of time but laughed it off when I was working all the time. But now these symptoms were in my face and I couldn't escape them or stay so busy that I couldn't go to the doctor. I remember my uncle Derry said to me that I didn't look well. It was different hearing it from him and the look on his face. You see my mother had been telling me I needed to go to the doctor. But she was harsh and scared me the way she said it. She said if you don't go to the doctor you are going to die. So, when she said it, I dismissed it and pushed it out of my mind. My niece Kennedy was a little girl at the time and she said auntie why your eyes are sticking out? My nephew Jordan hugged me and said, "Auntie" I feel your bones. It was almost towards the last day of my job. A few weeks later it was over. That awesome job I had was gone. They did however provide me with a

huge severance check. Few days later while watching a Jaguar football game, my heart start racing again, and I was extremely cold. But this time was different. I started to feel like I was blacking out. I knew to tell my husband to dial 911. And he did. The paramedics came and put a heart monitor on me and in a matter of minutes, I was on a gurney and they were racing me to the nearest hospital. They were on line with the hospital telling them how many minutes away we were. Then this guy pulled out this huge syringe full of medicine. I tried to negotiate my way out of them sticking me with it. I kept saying I am good. I am ok. You don't have to stick me. So, one paramedic said she appears pretty strong reach back here and squeeze my hand young lady. I looked backed to squeeze his hand to show how strong I was, and the other paramedic stuck that big needle in my arm. I found out later it is something that is done to reset your heart. I was diagnosed with Graves' disease which is an overactive thyroid issue. I was also diagnosed as anemic (Low-blood). I know that if I had been working still, I probably would have been at work when my heart started to feel funny and wouldn't have went to the doctor. Working so much caused a lot of medical issues that I had to get worse. My thyroid issue was taken care of and I take iron pills and vitamins for the low blood. I am so thankful to God for his grace and mercy. He took care of my son for me when I was lost. I am so proud of the man my son Jecoby has become. I know now, and I tell others. You can only serve one God. I found another job a few weeks later. Everything happens in our lives for a reason. When one door shut there is always another one to open. I thought that job was everything. It wasn't! God is everything. We can easily get lost and caught up. But don't ever thank that God has abandon you. He is always with you. He is working on your behalf behind the scene. Please don't get held hostage by a job. I can tell you some stories about corporate America. I have a book expected to be released in early 2019. Poisoned by Corporate America. It is a fiction and it will take you there. May God bless you and keep you. Stay in touch!

Towanda Young

Representing: Jamaica

Paperclip – Dreams Trapped Behind A Desk!

Have you ever felt stuck? Trapped? Unchallenged? Disengaged? Useless? Ignored? Lost? These are the feelings that many are feeling, doing something just to help them survive. My working life in the corporate world began as soon as I finished college. My first job was amazing! It was working for a well-known Union and the working conditions were great. I felt happy that I was brave enough to go for it. You see, I wasn't always the confident woman I am today. Years of negativity had taken its toll on my confidence to speak and my low self-esteem kept me bound.

The bullying from my school days didn't go away that easily. A lot of it was from my environment where I listened to others and their opinion. I then in turn began to believe the negative talk and played it over in mind, causing self-afflicted harm as well. This is something that is killing dreams. It's stopping people from going after their dreams and living the lives they were sent here to live. None of us are here by accident. Of the trillion chances of you being the one fertilized egg chosen, you and I have beaten the odds. Of all the things that could have happened during that conception period, you and I made it. There I said it, no one is an accident!

After leaving college, I was determined to get an apprenticeship in Business Administration. I was so happy when I saw the position advertised at the local job center. I jumped on the opportunity and went for it. I quickly asked the job center to put me forward for the position and they sent my details over to them. The following week the job center confirmed a morning interview with them. I was happy, and things were looking up. When you put your mind to it you can achieve anything.

On entering the gates, I was filled with excitement as the place was just so beautiful. I felt proud that there was a possibility that I might be working here. On arrival, I signed in and was asked to wait in the bar area. After about five minutes a lady, called Helen, came to get me and we went downstairs to her office. All of the offices and the print room were downstairs. The interview was very relaxed and more of a chat. I could tell that all was well from her reaction, but to stay with protocol, she said she would call me if I was accepted as an apprentice.

At the time, I was still living at my Step Grandad house, still waiting to get my own place. I had been on the housing list for a while, but nothing suitable was coming up which was worrying me. I wasn't happy living at my Granma's house as it wasn't the same. She had passed away and not having her around anymore was hard. Living with my Step Grandad wasn't easy. He was of the older generation with very set ways and opinions of how things should and shouldn't be. My Granma had my back when she was alive and now, she wasn't around anymore. Things got difficult.

I was there in my room when I heard the phone ring, the same afternoon of the interview. I rushed downstairs to answer it. It was the best news ever. Helen was on the other end telling me that they wanted me to do a Business Administration apprenticeship with them. I couldn't believe it. This was exactly what I wanted. This job had a starting salary of £8000 per annum, but it also had other perks such as pay raises, as you progress with the union. Other perks such as help with childcare would also cause an increase in the amount each month. And each year I got more and more!

When I first came to England, I would often tell my Aunt that I would work in an office one day and here it was coming to past! Words are powerful and everything that you seek in life is seeking you whether you know it or not. The words we speak have power and most people don't understand or know this to be so. When I was younger, I was a lot thinner. I was able to look at food without adding a pound onto my hips! So being a lover of food without piling on the pounds back then was music to my ear. But now working somewhere with unlimited amount of food is another story. We had many tea breaks as everything was there for us. Trust me this was a great place to be in. We were based at the training college in Whalley Range. We were in a beautiful building, on beautiful grounds as it stands today. The garden and the grounds were kept immaculate. The area of the grounds was so peaceful, and many hours were lost with long lunches here and there. I remember going for the interview. It was a lovely spring day. I felt positive as I had done my homework and learnt some information about the union for the interview to be prepared for questioning.

I embraced the opportunity and learnt some great skills whilst doing the job as it was very varied. One day I would be on reception duty. The next day I could be serving in the bar, or processing bookings for companies wanting to use the college for their events on another day. We were based downstairs in the events office and that's where I started my journey in the events world! I loved ensuring that they got a good service when planning their events. My greatest satisfaction came from knowing that everything went smoothly, and everything exceeded their expectations.

Jade and I developed a close friendship and boy we had some fun in that place. We had a thing for giant croissants. She would buy them on her way to work for us to have breakfast at our desks. She knew I had a thing for custard creams, so she would always dig through the vast amount of biscuits in the dining area to find my favorites. She was and still is a great friend with a very kind heart. She took me under her wings and nurtured me with her great administrative skills.

I was the youngest in the team at the age of twenty and it felt great being the baby of the team. The December after I started was my 21st birthday and boy did they go all out for it. I got to work, and my desk was covered with cards, flowers and gifts. I was spoilt rotten on my big day. We went to a local Chinese restaurant to celebrate and I had an amazing time with plenty of laughter.

I prayed for the perfect place to live, as I needed to leave my Granma's house to spread my wings. I made it a mission that I wanted to get my own place before my 22nd birthday and the summer before my birthday, I was offered a flat literally 5 minutes from my workplace. It was just the next street away. I was so happy that yet again just as I had asked it was given. I received exactly what I wanted. Whalley Range was now my home and my place of work. This made me feel happy and content. Working only a few minutes away from my home was great. I didn't have a long morning commute to get to work as it was less than five minutes away.

Becoming a mother!

It was the summer of 1999 when I met him. I remember him walking into the shop, I was young and shy. I would grab the one stare and then look away. It wasn't a love at first sight scenario. I would get excited when he came in the shop though and the staring would continue. One day after many visits he got the courage to ask for my number, which I couldn't even write because I was so nervous. I kept wandering if I gave him my number would he call. Yes, he did call, and we chatted, we arranged a date and that was how it all started. We would go to town, mostly in spinning fields, as there was a Spanish bar at the time that played great music with great vibes!

The courting began, and I got pregnant in the August of 2000. We had spent Christmas in Jamaica 1999 and our relationship grew from strength to strength. On our trip to Jamaica I wasn't well. I was bitten by some ants and the area got infected before I was due back in England. I had many doctor visits in Ocho Rios and he was there

every step of the way helping and looking after me. He made sure I was ok. He made sure I had everything that I needed. Even when I got back from the trip, I hadn't recovered fully, and I ended up in hospital. I was at work one day at the College and I felt poorly, and I mean really poorly. I felt weak and helpless and was rushed to the hospital. After several test at the hospital I was given antibiotics and was sent home. Once the antibiotics kicked in, I started to feel better.

> I prayed to have a little girl before I was twenty-five and I had her when I was twenty-three. Not having any of my close family in England left a void in my life but the birth of our little girl was a joyous moment.
>
> During my pregnancy, I felt awful and going into work was just as bad. I remember walking into the office with Julia asking me what was wrong. I was so pale, and I vomited everywhere. I got to work and swiftly I would have to dash to the toilet.
>
> I remember phoning my Mom in Jamaica to tell her I was pregnant, to which her response was about time! I was shocked at that, as I didn't know that my Mom was longing to see me have my own child. By this time, we moved to a bigger place which was big enough for the three of us. All the way through the pregnancy I was sick with one thing or another. The headaches were the worst and the swollen feet. I craved all sort of weird things that I wouldn't normally eat like figs. I'd never eaten them before I was pregnant. I had a thing for smells too and hated a particular aftershave. The smell would make me feel nauseous. To me it absolutely stunk, and the smell of the aftershave, even until today, still brings back that nauseous feeling.
>
> My maternity leave was four months full pay which was what I took and went back to work after five months. It was a struggle to put her

in childcare, so my Mom was more than happy to come to England for six months to look after her whilst I went back to work. My Mom loved her time in England and took the best care of her granddaughter. It was great having her here. I would get home and the house would be spotless, with dinner all cooked and ready. As mothers do, she took good care of us and it was great for her and Dellea to bond from such a young age. It's a bond that they still have today. She loves her Nanna as she calls her. I am so grateful that my Mom was able to come and help me out at a time when I really needed her. A mother's love is always there, and it doesn't matter whether they are near or far, it's a never-ending love!

After the six months, my mom had to go back to Jamaica. This was a task of getting a Toffler to nursery every morning before going to work. I was across the other side of town, so I had to catch two busses every morning, one to town and then the 86 bus to Whalley Range. It wasn't easy as I was on my own with little support.

Moving On!

February 2004 was the year that things would change as it was when the news of the College closure came. I was in this job five years now and really enjoyed working there. I got worried about finding another job, but I trusted and prayed to get something just as good or better.

"All you can possibly need, or desire is already yours, call your desires into being by imagining and feeling your wish fulfilled" Neville Goddard (1905-1972) New Thought Author.

I started on the mission of finding a job in time without a long break between. I saw this as an opportunity to move forward and didn't think of it as the worst thing that could have happened.

As a first proper job, I couldn't have asked for better. I met some amazing people whilst working there, some of which I still see today.

Your reaction to situations and how you view things, will determine the outcome. Not all situations are bad! When things happen it's your guide to your greater purpose and is part of your journey.

After checking the papers every day, I spotted an advert for a position with a local government organization. I wasn't sure I would get this position, but I started to believe that I would and started the task of getting it. I contacted the number listed and requested an application pack. When it arrived in the post, it was long with plenty to go through. With perseverance I completed it and returned it. After a few weeks to my delight I got a letter telling me that I was shortlisted and got an interview. I was so happy that I had gotten this far in the process.

For the interview I made sure that I researched the organization and what they did. Well that was scary as that was when I realized the enormity of what they did. This was an organization working with local councils and the government nationally, with a vast amount of local government employees in its membership! Wow, I thought how would little old me get into an organization like this?

My dream has always been to one day study a degree course, but circumstances didn't allow it at the time. Plus, I had no confidence that it was something that I could achieve, as I didn't think I was bright enough. Never let anyone tell you that you cannot achieve something!

The day of the interview came, and I was nervous, very nervous. All sorts of things were going around in my head wondering what they would ask me. I was confident that I had researched the organization, but I wasn't sure of the other questions that they would ask me. I knew where the building was, as I had driven passed it several times, not knowing what businesses were based there. The office was situated on the second floor of one of the office blocks. On arrival, I reported to the reception and was directed to where the interview was being held.

I was greeted by a lovely lady, of which today she is still in my life and has been a great support. I really connected with her and we got along great. I could relate to her in so many ways. The interview went great and I was proud of how I answered the questions. The Chief Executive seemed happy and all I had to do now was wait for that call. The afternoon of the interview I got a call from the lovely lady telling me that I had got the job and a letter of offer will be sent, formally offering me the post. YES! I thought I did it! I asked, and I received. I wanted to start another job without any gap that was what I would be doing.

After I received the offer letter, I told my colleagues at the College and they thought I was lucky in finding another position so quick. To myself, I was thinking that it had nothing to do with lucky, as it was my prayers being answered!

I started my new chapter on the 14 March 2004. It was just ideal with the opportunity to travel. After my induction training, I started to learn more about the organization and who was in it. After some months in the role things changed, as the office manager's responsibility change and the management of the team transferred to someone else. I wasn't happy with this change. I knew that the person managing the team would be a nightmare. From observing her in the office, I knew that she didn't have the attitude of a good manager. I noticed how she often dropped comments here and there that would make you cringe. I quickly noticed how she wasn't genuine to people that were different from her and certain comments she made were totally off limits. My gut instincts took me back to the bullying that I endured in school. I loved the job, but she often criticized my skills and understanding of things. She would blatantly bully a specific team member and I wondered why it wasn't spotted by management. She had their full support when she raised issues against him. I could easily tell that she just didn't like him, and she was going to make his working life unbearable.

I spotted the signs and took him under my wings like a younger brother, as I hated the way he was being treated. Deep down I think the reason she got away with so much was the fact that she worked closely with those in higher positions within the organization. Things started to become very regimented, especially when we were working away at seminars. I was terrified of the people in higher positions and had no confidence around them. My confidence was being squashed every day. I felt lost at times and as time went by things didn't get any better.

I knew that, like many, they would strategically manage us and eventually we'd bout be out the door in time to come. I remember being at a seminar in Blackpool and realized that they didn't care whether the staff had a break or had something to eat. One of the worse things was sitting in the restaurant rushing to have something to eat because I was feeling so weak. As soon as I sat down, I was told that I had to get back to work. This was really upsetting because I knew that without the staff, the seminar couldn't continue so they are just as important as the delegates.

>As time went by, I didn't like what I was seeing. I knew that things were changing, and I often felt out of place. The fact that I was the only black employee made things even worse. I hated the jokes and certain things that my manager would try and repeat to make words sound Jamaican. Until today, I hate, that beer can joke. My manager used it regularly to get people laughing in the office.

>I wanted to achieve so much more in that organization as over the years I'd applied for positions hoping to progress to the next level.
>It wasn't meant to be. I showed that I wanted to progress by applying for several vacancies as they became available. By this time, I had a new manager and new people that joined the team, so things were a little more bearable, or so I thought at the times. But one particular team member that joined was destined to make my life a living hell. I really felt hated by her and straight away I knew she would become part of the reason I would eventually leave. I knew

that any position that becomes available she stood more chances of getting it, more than me.

In my one to one and appraisals, no progression route were ever discussed. I knew that I was a big asset to the organization, but I guess I was just fulfilling their diversity quota. I had the potential just like everyone else in the team, but due to their narrow minds, I never stood a chance. I started to realize that I would never progress any further in that post. I was frightened to do anything about it. After all, I had family responsibilities as we had a new addition to our family May 2011. Aljay arrived, but not much changed after coming back from maternity leave.

I even continued studying and successfully completed a home study course in Management Studies. But I guess that wasn't even considered when considering my hunger to progress. When I look back, I can truly see how I was held back in so many ways. I think even though I gave so much in all, that I did whilst in that job. Half the time I truly did feel like a paperclip. Just the girl or woman holding things together. Because of the length of time I had worked there, everyone would ask me rather than ask anyone else. I was the go-to girl in the office and as much as I love stationery, I really hated spending my time counting paperclips and tipex.

After giving birth to my twins in 2014 my return following my maternity was when I started to realize that it was my time to be managed out the door and so it was. Once I got back into the job I quickly noticed how much had changed and how little I was left with. My job had been given to the same person that hated me. She was now in charge of the major conferences and all the ones that were designated to me throughout the year. Attendance at major seminars and meetings were no longer part of my role. Diary management, booking travel arrangements were gone too. To top it off, that same person was promoted into a completely different role whilst I was on maternity leave. She received the progression that I had so desired. I am not sure if they knew how this was affecting me as no one sat down with me to tell me that half my job was gone. This was upsetting, and it affected me more than I realized at the time. I felt useless and it made me feel that all this happened because I am a woman who had children. It left me wondering 'why me' but I guess I knew the answer deep down. I realized it was time to move on. If they couldn't see my worth, that would be their loss. I know that I gave my all, but I guess that wasn't enough for them.

Things felt different and I knew better must come. To study and gain a degree was a lifelong dream. I didn't get to go to university after finishing college, so this was still on the list of achievements for me. Looking back now I am so grateful for all the things that happened in between that lead me to finally break free and leave where I was being tolerated. The decision to finally leave was one of my best yet. It started to make me ill and that was the last straw as my anxiety was getting worse. The days of pulling over on the road in tears was becoming more regular. I remember driving to work with tears streaming down my face to the point where I had to pull over and telephone work telling them I couldn't come into work. My husband was my rock as usual and his support was simply amazing. Having his shoulder to cry on was just what I needed at the time.

Whenever we talked about my situation, he would encourage me and knowing he had my back was the best feeling ever. I will forever be grateful for his love and support in everything that I do. Completing the university application was frightening but I knew I was doing the right thing and it had to be done. I owed it to myself to fulfil that dream of gaining my degree. I knew that I had to fulfil my purpose and staying in that job wasn't going to get me anywhere. At times you just got to move on and chase that dream. I felt let down in many ways as I know that I gave everything to that job, but I guess to them that wasn't enough. I was filled with fear, but I knew that I had to do it as I never stood a chance in progressing any further in my job. I often felt that I wasn't good enough because if I was, I would get the progression I deserved. The odds were stacked against me. I am a woman and a black one at that, and I had children. I knew that these factors were considered, and I never stood a chance no matter what institutional racism existed. Unfortunately for me that was how I started to see things.

> I submitted the university application on the Wednesday and the next day I received an unconditional offer from the university. I was so happy, and I knew it was the sign that I needed to confirm that I was doing the right thing. In life you have to learn to not just settle for the worth that others have tagged you with. You deserve more, and you can do more. It would have been an easy option to stay in that job until retirement but where would that get me? Leaving that job was a big decision but I would never have the opportunities that I have had since leaving it. I am now in the last year of my degree which has flown by quick. The journey has been empowering since leaving the job that wasn't going anywhere. The opportunities have been amazing. My message to anyone, stuck in a just to pay the bills, is that you need to work on your dreams and understand that you are worth so much more. Others won't see your worth until you do!
>
> Don't compromise your dreams and goals to just pay the bills. Your dreams are just as important as everyone else's.
>
> My message is, embrace opportunities and be grateful for how far you have come. No one can fulfill what you came here to do. Only you know!
>
> I am excited to develop my radio show and build on the global audience. Completing my upcoming book in which you can read more about my journey is my focus now. I have quite a few dreams and goals to achieve. so with grace and mercy I will be working on them.

Massive thanks to my amazing family, friends and all the people who supported me and continue to do so!

Representing: Haiti

From Secrets to Success Jacqueline Moise

The sexual abuse began in my early childhood and continued until my adult years for a little over seventeen years. By the time I was twelve years old, I was sexually assaulted by a neighbor, a close family friend, a door to door salesman, a stranger, and my very own father, when it all began. As I begin to write this story, my heart is beating rapidly and feeling doubtful that I can continue. I'm not very sure I possess the courage to disclose the events of my life as I can remember, however it's imperative that I break my silence before it breaks me.

For years, I had no idea that I was dealing with physical, psychological, emotional, and spiritual abuse. As a child, I learned to adapt to my environment, stay quiet and never embarrass the family in public with nonsense. My long journey began at the age of five after my mom and I left the poverty ridden country of Haiti. I was born in The Bahamas, but my mother had to leave shortly after I was born due to my grandfather's request for her to return to Haiti. He wasn't too fond of my father and was not happy with my mother and I living afar. My mother returned to Haiti so that her family could see me, the first grandchild in the family. She was so proud and excited about introducing me to everyone. A few months had passed, and my mother felt it was time for us to return to The Bahamas with me, but my grandfather had other plans. He kept my mother's passport and insisted that we stay. He believed he could do a better job at providing for us rather than my father. I really enjoyed living with my grandfather in Haiti and recall feeling safe and extremely happy with life. My aunt and uncles were much younger than my mother and just a few years older than me, so I had other kids my age to play with. We played outside every day for as long as we could before being called in for a bath and dinner. My family made life enjoyable and memorable during our stay in Haiti. Sundays were my favorite. My mother was a talented seamstress that designed signature dresses that I wore every

Sunday for church. We lived in Haiti until my grandfather was killed by Tontons Macoutes, Haiti's secret police force found by the dictator "Papa Doc" Francois Duvalier. A few months before my mother's visa would expire, my grandmother found our passports which enabled us to leave Haiti and return to The Bahamas.

Upon our arrival to The Bahamas, my father greeted us at the airport. I didn't know much about my father, but I was very excited to meet him for the first time. My quality of life in The Bahamas was not much like it in Haiti. As a child, it wasn't apparent that our economic status was that of poverty. At times, we didn't have electricity, water, or food, but amid this, it was reassuring to be in the presence of family. It was a joyous experience to have family sit in the living room with candles lit and listening to my father attempting to play his guitar and sing songs in both French and Spanish. I vividly recall this because I found it impressive that my dad spoke three languages, Spanish,

English and French. He was my hero. Our meals mostly came from the garden in the back of the house. Our garden consisted of corn, spinach like plants, a lot of greens and potatoes. Cooking meals was like camping out and having fun. My mom cooked our meals on a half-cut barrel used as a substitute for a stove and I knew no different.

Then that day One day came. My father told me that this is how people show each other love. What I had to do to show I loved him because he loved me. My first of many blow job… I complied because I wanted my father to know that I do love him. He also added that this was a secret and not to tell anyone especially my mother because she would be very jealous.

My second encounter was a door to door salesman that my mother seemed to trust. He came over to the house often selling a variety of items to my mom. It seemed like she trusted him, so the day he came to the door when my parents weren't home was no different. He asked that I open the door because he had a surprise for me and I did. Again, another secret. My father introduced me to secrets and that made me feel special, but I didn't feel like I was. Sounds strange to say that thank God that he never made me have intercourse with me, just your normal everyday "blow job". It seemed like he would come around when my parents weren't home for some strange reason… One day, my mother happened to tell me not to let anyone in the house while she was gone. That was my saving grace. I didn't want to disrespect another adult by not doing what I'm told. When the salesman came to the door that day, I told him I was not allowed to open the door because my mother said so. He told me that my mother told him to come by to drop off some items and that I can open the door for him. Something in me gave me the strength to say NO, I can't. He became very upset, banging on the door and telling me I would get in trouble if I didn't open the door. I was so scared but did not open that door.

We moved to another house that had more kids in the neighborhood to play with. Little do they know, I'm a professional outside player…. I call myself having my first boyfriend name Michael. He happened to ride his bike in front of my house one day and said hello. That was the first boy my age that said hello to me and has never left my mind. He came around all the time just to play and talk with me. I loved Michael. Our neighbor was probably watching us when he mentioned to me that if I don't kiss him, he would tell my father I was playing with boys and would get in trouble. Michael was worth a kiss. I loved him, besides, our neighbor didn't ask me to do anything wrong. It was just a kiss... Crazy how innocence can hurt a child.

My family left The Bahamas and started living in Miami, FL. A new country. I was so excited to fly in a plane. This time I was five and old enough to enjoy the experience. A new place. My brother was born and now I'm a big sister after twelve years of being the only child. I had high hopes of new friends and no more secrets. I hate them. Well that was short lived. My next encounter was with my brother's godfather. I remember him being tall, lite skinned, soft hair and handsome. He took an interest in me. I'm supposed to feel happy right? By this time, my breast started getting a little fuller and now I'm a big girl. He explained to me this is what big girls do. He wanted to show me affection and that's "how big girls" show their affection. I wanted to show that I am a "big girl" and will do what it takes to do prove it and touching games was one way to show that. but why would he want to touch me when there's no one around? I wanted everyone to know that I was a "big girl" now. Here we go again, it had to be a secret because people would be jealous, and I didn't want that. Again, there was no intercourse or "blow jobs". How "lucky" was I?

I missed the bus one day on my way from school and this white man drove up saw that I missed the bus and offered to give me a ride to my connecting bus stop. That he does this all the time to help people out. How nice of him. On the way there, he asked me questions about school, friends and family that made me feel safe at the time. Besides, I was never told not to ride with strangers. He was helping me get home in time after missing my bus. He got me to my bus stop like he said he would and told me that there was a small fee. It wouldn't take long. I said ok what is it. He wanted me to touch his penis and just stroke it up and down for him. So, I did. Not like he was asking for much, you think? I was able to catch my bus and get home on time and never spoke a word about it to anyone. Never did he ask me to keep it a secret, so I guess it was ok, right?

Things got stressful after my family became homeless. Moving all the time. Place to place. School to school. I was unable to have long time friendships because of that. We finally moved to Brooklyn, NY and shortly afterwards my sister was born. I had to ensure that I protected her from everything and everyone. Felt like that was my duty. At this time, I started junior high school and excelled. School came easy to me. It was the perfect hiding place. A place to get

away and be with friends, learn new things, play, and most importantly, feel safe. There was no escaping after get home. My father visited my room at least once a week mostly at night when my mother was working. I wished he wouldn't. My father frequently threatens my mother's life and to leave the family if I ever told anyone. I began to think this was all my fault. The day I lost my virginity to my father was the worst day of my life. I said The Lord's Prayer during the ordeal, hoping God would save me. But no answer. I felt angry, upset, depressed, hurt, anxious, sad and betrayed. Now, I am not a virgin when I get married. Thoughts of shame, and disgust filled my head. I started having nightmares, couldn't focus in school, and the things I enjoyed doing the most were a now a burden. I started stealing alcohol from the house and drinking a lot to numb the pain. Playing sports keep my interest. I played sports all throughout high school just, so I don't have to go home early. Didn't feel safe. Sports became my escape from reality. I never played organized sports before, but I soon found out I was a natural. It also gave me a sense of belonging to a group of true individuals that really cared for me with no strings attached. I played three different sports, basketball, volleyball, and softball, with three different coaches that are some of the best people that made a huge impact in my life. They trained and influenced us in a way that that tested my character, build inner strength and decision making all at the same time. I am for sure, that's where the seed of a voice was planted in me to have the courage to speak and take action.

The courage to fight, and the courage to feel strong. It was a very strange feeling at first, but it became addictive.

The abuse continued into my twenties. I had to leave home. I had to leave Brooklyn. My new-found courage led me to join the United States Navy a few years later but I stilled lack the voice of courage to stand up to my father. It was deeply rooted. My passion for courage and to let others know to have and use their courage drove me to have a very successful twenty-seven

years in the Navy. Soon after joining, I was pregnant with my son and called home to tell them the great news. The news was not so welcoming because I was not married at the time. The plan for my boyfriend and I to get married was planned for a later date. I went home for my thirty days leave where I was again assaulted by my father. My courage had not been tested in this matter ever since leaving home and I failed. Failed to protect myself and my unborn son. This caught me off guard. Shame, disgust, pain and defeat possessed me once more. I was conflicted. I hated myself. I eventually told my mother about what had happened. It felt good to not be hiding it anymore. They soon divorced. I wanted nothing but to be normal and happy again.

July came, and God gave me my Son, my miracle. My emotions were unfamiliar to me in the most amazing way. I am so grateful for him. Now I'm a mother. Everything must change both internal and external. I must protect my son and my family from my father. Courage must take over once again. Now it's not just for me, it's for my son!

My journey has molded me to who I am today. For that, I am grateful. I'm a survivor. From the outside world I was an educated woman, that was successful in whatever career I chose to pursue. I concealed my abuse by wearing many hats consisting of being a mother, a daughter, a sister, a girlfriend, a friend, a professional and now a grandmother. Each day, I encounter many triggers and flashbacks that will cause me to switch hats to be able to get through the day. I had to ensure that everything I did was perfect. No failure allowed in anything I do. Others will come to know my secret that may lead me to sabotage.

God placed great people in my life who have helped me in my healing along the way many of whom have no idea what they done for me. I can't erase all that has happened to me, but I can give a voice to others with similar pain. Feeling of lost. Feeling dirty, ashamed, weak and hopeless sharing my story. I may had healed on the outside, but there's still a wounded child that

> still reside within my soul. The difference is, that child knows she's in a safe place. That it's okay to come out and be innocent, happy, and carefree.
>
> Years ago, I first heard the term "sharing is caring" from the little sister and I thought that was so simple but profound. So, I bring that to you. In sharing my story with others, I realized that I was facing my deepest fear. The fear of people finding out about my shame, feeling of being embarrassed, and their judgements. I began to feel connected to my purpose in life. My calling to empower others, both men and women. I never knew innocent boys and young men were suffering through those same predicaments. Removing the feeling of isolation, internal suffering, darkness and despair.
>
> Through pain, came success. My grandson was born with hydrocephalus which came with several health-related challenges. A new lifelong friend and business partner recommended that I invested in my grandson's health with Hydrogen Enriched Water to see if that will help with some of his many challenges. At the time, I was willing to try anything to improve his quality of life. A simple water test revealed that the bottled baby water we were using was very acidic. Very low alkaline levels that increased the acid levels in his stomach. Once I changed his water, it changed his life. He looked healthy, full of life and awakened. It didn't take long before I became an Independent Distributor. Now I run a successful business educating others in the importance of quality of water. Hydrogen Enriched Water is an alternative to pharmaceutical drugs. It can assist others with a better way of life drug free, mentally, physically, and

emotionally by improving the quality of water people consume. We can change the world and we can start by simply improving the quality our water.

An Enagic Independent Distributor

A Foreign Exchange (FOREX) and Crypto Currency Trader / Network Marketer

Representing: Kenya East Africa

When I Gave My Life and Heart to The Lord

My name is Gilbert Wanyonyi and I'm from Bungoma Kenya East Africa. I was born in nineteen seventies to government working, teaching parents. Life to me was not all that way hard compared to most in my village. My colleagues and I had a bright future together with my **siblings**. It was in my final year of high school, when preparing to write for my final exams, that I began experiencing some sharp persistent headaches. I went for medical assistance, concerning the headaches for quite a while, but they couldn't help me. Instead of getting better, my condition worsened. The remaining of the year was no pleasant. I had very bad pain and this was the time of year I should have been enjoying maturing into my new season with my colleagues. Bedridden at this point, I could only sit back and watch my colleagues begin school at the university and tertiary college's. Not only were the headaches increasing but I was now paralyzed on my left side, limbs and all with blurred vision.

In my country when the doctors can't help you, people oftentimes seek help from other means. Well the doctors weren't helping my situation and I didn't want to end this way. I knew I had more life in me and I would do anything at this point to get healed so I sought out help from a witch doctor with my parents help. Seems extreme, but as a young man, I just wanted to live, and this was the way I knew others had gone and at times received help for their condition.

After visiting the witch doctor and finding they too could not find a remedy to help me. One might give up hope and though it was hard and seemed hopeless at times I still couldn't give up. I remembered hearing others talk about God. The doctors couldn't help me. The witch doctors couldn't help me. Just maybe the Lord could help me. Well, this route wouldn't come easy as I decided to seek the Lord. Word spread, and false prophets and pastors were lined up before me saying they were sent by God and had the answer. They had been sent by Satan to detour me from my healing. The more I studied and learned of the Lord, I began to see the TRUTH. I could see and differentiate between the fake from the real pastors and ministries. God was shining upon me and bringing me sight in the spiritual and natural realms, in that order.

> It was realized that I'd had a stroke and the Lord had healed me. This is when I gave the Lord my all. I gave the lord my heart and strength. No one could help and heal me but HIM. HE had healed me from my stroke. Praise God from Whom All Blessings Flow. After the miracle that had taking place in my physical body and my inner mind, my commitment would be shown when I joined biblical college instead of secular one. You would think that with such great news and miracle in my life my family and friends would rejoice with me. But no, this was the beginning of another bad situation as I was rejected and lost the favor of my parents' siblings, and friends in my village. It was one thing to claim healing but another thing to say you are giving your all to this God and turn from the plans we'd made for secular university and now you're going to this biblical school. My parents and siblings were my financial support, and all of this would be cut off. Times now became hard, not because of illness, but due to finances. With this rejection, I was stressed, confused, and feeling alone. BUT just as HE'd shown up for me to heal me, the Lord came to see me through. After seeing all that the Lord was doing in my life and how the blessings were flowing, the Lord allowed my parents to favor me again and restored our relationship. I got a girl and she is

now my wife. Our children are now in high school. I'm blessed with a ministry as well. FACT: The Lord is faithful to his children. I have seen him saving, healing and bringing restoration in my life, family and ministry as well. TRUTH: He'll do the same for you.

Representing: Canada

Be the Change - Christopher Braeuel

Now approaching 50, I look back at my life and think about that one night in 1988 when I saw my first Up With People (UWP) performance in Ottawa, Canada, and how it determined the rest of my life. There I was at the end of the show, sitting in my theatre seat, totally overwhelmed and not wanting to leave. The many young members, all coming from different parts of the world, singing and dancing like professionals, I just couldn't believe what I had seen.

When the invitation for an interview was announced I stayed with quite a few others. It was the time before cell phones, and when I finally got home at 1 a.m. my worried parents had already called the police. They forgave me however and supported me through all the rest of the preparations, especially the fundraising. They were as excited as I when they heard more about this international educational organization whose mission was to bridge cultural barriers and create global understanding through community service. Over one year 120 selected students from 20 nations, travel as a group to over 14 countries. My parents even flew to Tucson a few months after I left home to see my team off when it started for New Mexico after much amazing, Hollywood-aided preparation, for its first public performance. They came as well to see us in Vermont. And what a thrill it was for me when all relatives of the German side of my family, including my grandparents, saw my group in Goslar as we were covering that country too. We performed in Berlin when the wall came down, an unforgettable experience! It was a fantastic feeling to see the excitement we caused wherever we went that year. I will never forget it, it is hard to describe. By that time, you realize that you have met a great number of people and learned to be comfortable with them. You realize that you have the power to make them happy, that you can do a lot more than you think you can. You realize that you perhaps can make a difference. My love for travel too had been awakened, and I was ready to make the world a better place.

But to do this well I thought it would be a good idea to first invest a few years of studying. I finished with a combined BA Honors in History and Public Management and a master's in public administration. It was the millennium now and the field of international development interested me. Eighteen years of progressive experience in project and program management followed, providing me with immense satisfaction and showing me that those years in university had been worthwhile. Here are a few descriptions of time frames and destinations:

I represented Canada in the United Nations in 2008 as Chief Advisor and Bureau Vice-President to the UN Convention to combat Desertification. In Buenos Aires, while at a conference, I met a lovely lady who was representing Latvia and who would a few years later become my wife.

From 2009 to 2012, I worked with the Canadian Embassy in Kabul where I managed Canada's support to Afghanistan's education sector. Nobody needs much imagination to realize that it was sometimes hard on the emotions to see the desperate need for rehabilitation of the schools. We found indescribable conditions. Especially the utter hopelessness of a certain school for the blind. I will never be able to forget.

There is much more to my story that I hope to share in a more detailed book in the future.

"Fight to win" is the message and the moral of my story. I've always thought that Fighting to win was an ingrained or natural inclination. I never thought that fighting to win was something that needed to be taught or encouraged. I believed that Fighting to win was a part of a human's most powerful survival instinct. As if fighting to win was some sort of default setting in our personal programming. Yet, there are many people in this world who are fighting battles daily without any intention of winning. There are even people who commit spiritual suicide by deliberately self-sabotaging any hope of victory but Why? What's stopping these people from putting forth a winning effort? Some people won't give winning efforts because they don't think their battles can be won. So, they chose to give up and lose by default.

In our Daily lives, we are constantly fighting our own personal battles. Battles that are as unique as a fingerprint. Personal battles can happen to anyone in all areas of our life with various combinations and levels of intensity. These battles usually take place in three main area: our minds, our bodies, and our spirit. When life's battles are happening simultaneously in all three those main areas, life can get very tough. But if we allow personal battles to overwhelm us with stress and worry. The littlest things seem massive and the simplest problems seem complex. Our imagination can skew our visions of future. But no matter the variation, combination or intensity of battle, we must still fight and fight to win.

There are people who have been convinced that they can't win their personal battles and as result, they are ready to give up and quit fighting a battle that could be well within their grasp. Maybe they feel as if they have nothing to fight for or they have nothing to fight with or they just feel like they are fighting all alone... if this is you then my message to you is: continue to fight and fight to win.

Faith creates motivation. Motivation creates momentum. Momentum creates movement and it becomes a move of faith. When we fight to win, we are moving by faith.

KINGS KID - FLORIDA

CARPENTER'S KID   - Transparency4Souls

"The Gift of Conviction" - A Matter of The Heart

I could talk about coming through life from a divorced household or becoming a divorcee and single mother. Or I could even talk about my life after being hit by a vehicle while walking across the street in a cross walk, which was my intended story, But not this time.
I realize through the creation of this first anthology, A Winning World, life has a way of blindsiding you when you least expect it. Or is it that, if GOD had shown me what was up ahead in saying YES to this project, I may have aborted the mission and said NO WAY? God has a way of changing the program. Not to say HE chose the road I'd walk in any way, but HE knew I'd come to a cross roads that would either make or break me, showing what I was made of. Or better yet, HE turns our bad choices around for our good when we haven't fully trusted HIM, though we thought we are trusting HIM.

We all have the best intentions I believe, but it's a choice and matter of the heart that gives you the outcome of being a winner or loser, NO MATTER HOW GRIM IT MAY SEEM in some seasons.

I also realize no matter where we are in this world, we are more alike than different, and face many of the same challenges. If we can embrace this, I believe we'll become more unified and can begin to build our world together, rather than seeing differences and tearing it down and a part.

Some of us believe in different things and stand upon different beliefs and lifestyles. It's beautiful when we can share stories of how we've come through trials, overcome, to living victorious lives to help build others who will read or hear of the stories we've shared here. My story will be that of my faith in God, but lack of trust, my belief, and how I was raised, which foundation ultimately steered me back to victory. How I fail in a moment in flesh(sin), realizing this battle would truly be for my soul (a spiritual battle) in this mission to build others, and how I overcame to live triumphantly in my truth to help others do the same. Though it was a set up from the enemy and this person had planned every move, I played a part in walking into the trap. I would come face to face with things within me that had never been revealed, drawing me closer to God.

I was broken and had a sense of insecurity after becoming disabled physically. I didn't realize the degree of my silent suffering until facing this I'll share here in this, my story.

Psalm 23 (KJV)

23 The LORD is my shepherd; I shall not want. [2] He maketh me to lie down in green pastures: he leadeth me beside the still waters. [3] He restoreth my soul: he leadeth me in the paths of righteousness for his name's sake. [4] Yea, though I walk through the valley of the shadow of death, I will fear no evil: for thou art with me; thy rod and thy staff they comfort me. [5] Thou preparest a table before me in the presence of mine enemies: thou anointest my head with oil; my cup runneth over. [6] Surely goodness and mercy shall follow me all the days of my life: and I will dwell in the house of the LORD forever.

I'm choosing to share my story as a minister of the WORD, from a pastor's perspective, and the pain associated in falling to sin. But keep in mind this is not just about people with titles. We all have a mission in life and fall short at times through distractions or misfortunes. This oftentimes causes us to fail to focus and see our dreams or purpose through. Life's errors can take our eyes off the prize, no matter what seat we may sit in or positions we may hold.

I've seen it and heard how leaders stumble and how the fall can destroy them and has destroyed ministries and lives. And thus, the fear of sharing goes without saying, it has been the detriment to many because they failed to see the perfect God loving our imperfections through Grace and Mercy to redemption. Fear itself has no place in The Kingdom but is often the thing used to tie up the lives of the believer, causing them to suffer alone, silently, and condemned. It also is the most kept secret and can be a tormenting hell in the mind when you must carry such burden of hiding because there is no outlet. As it was in the day of Jezebel when she had brought in fear in the land and the prophets were hidden in caves verses realizing the Great God within them. Also, as a woman, society has been much harsher on her than the male counter part holding her to a higher standard versus realizing, life situations can bring you to a place you'd never imagine. This was in biblical times too when they brought forth the woman to stone her, but left the man out of the picture and Jesus began to write in the sand, ALL sins all have committed at some point and they had to walk away leaving her unharmed.

I truly can relate to how Adam must have felt when he realized he was naked. He had everything in his hand, at his request. I often wonder, what was his distraction. The fact that he hid himself is proof that sin is what causes fear. Another fact and the greatest to hold, is that repentance gives hope, hope brings forth LIFE as you grab a hold of the Truth in Faith, Believing. God sent Adam and Eve away clothed but yet they had lost that freedom of having all at their fingertips without care or concern.

Isaiah 41:10 | KJV
Fear thou not; for I am with thee:
be not dismayed; for I am thy God: I will
strengthen thee; yea, I will help thee;
yea, I will uphold thee with the right hand of my righteousness.

I have been in a process for a while to create a safe-haven for leaders in the FAITH, since the death of a well-known pastor, whom I loved, he and his wife dearly. I'd go visit them because I was truly in awe of watching them minister together, as one. He'd talk and then she'd come in and add to it and it became a volley of sorts in sharing and ministering the WORD as a unit force. Oh, how I loved it. Well, he'd fall to temptation of a past addiction and exposure would come. He eventually ended up dying and never fully recovering from the hurt and shame of this affliction. Many ministers and leaders experience fall away due to something in them they've failed to face and not realizing the power within them to defeat the enemy, within, that has already been defeated on the cross. Maybe through pride or just not truly having a real relationship to understand that no matter how low you go, God is always there with open arms, filled with LOVE if we just repent, with Godly sorrow in heart, and a transformed mind to not go back into that we're set free from to be lifted up. The understanding of The FATHER's LOVE is everything and makes the difference on whether we run and hide or face and defeat the spirit that seeks to steal, kill, and destroy us, making us victorious. Judas and Peter are great examples of this. Judas betrayed Jesus and ended up killing himself. Peter denied Jesus and went away sorrowful, with a repentant heart and when Jesus arose from the dead, HE came asking, "where is Peter?" Quite amazing the revelation and difference God has given me concerning the differences between betrayal and denial, but we'll save that for another book.

Psalm 34 ESV

19 Many are the afflictions of the righteous, but the LORD delivers him out of them all.
20 He keeps all his bones; not one of them is broken.
21 Affliction will slay the wicked, and those who hate the righteous will be condemned.
22 The LORD redeems the life of his servants; none of those who take refuge in him will be condemned.

These stories of ministers falling away have always tugged at me. Time and time again, we see it happening all the time, playing out in the media, minister caught here, or minister did that. Or hear as I did in a service space, where members and others were talking verses getting with the person and praying or just believing for the soul and/or souls connected.

Psalm 91 (KJV)

91 He that dwelleth in the secret place of the most High shall abide under the shadow of the Almighty. [2] I will say of the LORD, He is my refuge and my fortress: my God; in him will I trust. [3] Surely he shall deliver thee from the snare of the fowler, and from the noisome pestilence. [4] He shall cover thee with his feathers, and under his wings shalt thou trust: his truth shall be thy shield and buckler.

⁵ Thou shalt not be afraid for the terror by night; nor for the arrow that flieth by day; ⁶ Nor for the pestilence that walketh in darkness; nor for the destruction that wasteth at noonday. ⁷ A thousand shall fall at thy side, and ten thousand at thy right hand; but it shall not come nigh thee. ⁸ Only with thine eyes shalt thou behold and see the reward of the wicked. ⁹ Because thou hast made the LORD, which is my refuge, even the most High, thy habitation; ¹⁰ There shall no evil befall thee, neither shall any plague come nigh thy dwelling. ¹¹ For he shall give his angels charge over thee, to keep thee in all thy ways. ¹² They shall bear thee up in their hands, lest thou dash thy foot against a stone. ¹³ Thou shalt tread upon the lion and adder: the young lion and the dragon shalt thou trample under feet. ¹⁴ Because he hath set his love upon me, therefore will I deliver him: I will set him on high, because he hath known my name. ¹⁵ He shall call upon me, and I will answer him: I will be with him in trouble; I will deliver him, and honour him. ¹⁶ With long life will I satisfy him, and shew him my salvation.

Now one would think that because this has been a focal point of mine, that it's no way, I would find myself in this kind of situation, and I would have agreed, but it's not how it happened, not how it played out for my life. I found myself one day walking right into the lion's den. Yes, I did not fall into sin, I walked into it. The person had, what seemed to be all the check points that said you could trust his actions and feel safe. Businessman, making life happen, and SOMEONE TO BUILD AN EMPIRE WITH WHILE HELPING OTHERS if God allowed it to go that way.

Now with this statement alone, my focus had been clouded, because the only empire I should ever be concerned with is building that of the Kingdom of God, but I somehow in this place and space mixed the two. I was trying to rebuild my life financially and physically, currently. I had many hits, but my physical hit was a huge blow. My eyesight shifted from Kingdom viewpoint to world view as my trust was failing unknown to me. I saw no money in my account, but God was providing. I could work and saw money coming in, money to provide, I could see to take care of me and my family. At this point, though God was providing, I focused on what I couldn't see happening, therefore the scripture on faith is the substance of things hoped for, the evidence of things not seen, was not in action in my life. I focused on what I could do to make connections and making money verses resting in the fact that God would provide and was providing.

Well, I met McCoy, the branding expert (later to be discovered Predator in disguise). We talked daily and though something inside said caution, I was ready for something to change and maybe he could help. Mind you, I was hurting, broken, medicating pain, and seeing someone accepting me with my healing limitations was seemingly a great place to be in. He came with a story as well and appeared very sincere. Though I was putting on my smiling face outwardly, praying and ministering to others almost daily, I was losing myself. Depression had set in but being that I'd never known depression and doctors were saying I was I rebuked the statements. I felt if I spoke it, it would become my reality. I'd cry at moments when there was nothing to cry about, just sitting and tears would flow. Or I start thinking on my accident and all the changes that had occurred with tears, but I thought it's normal to feel sad occasionally. My business was booming at the time of the accident. I was making more money doing what I truly enjoyed. Buying what I wanted to buy, living like I wanted to live with my children. This, coupled with medication, had me in a place of asking God at times, if you will let me know my children will be okay, YOU can let me sleep away. I had moments of not wanting to wake up. I wasn't suicidal but just was in so much pain and stressed, I just wanted to sleep on if God allowed. This was Depression. So, conversation with someone that wasn't screaming, arguing, yelling, fueling my pain points, etc. was welcomed in any form this juncture in my life. He'd shared enough of his childhood and life that I thought he was open and honest. He even gave me a book he'd written that outlined pretty much everything he was sharing, as well as some added stuff. Seemed impressive to the ear and eye and it blended with my new created purpose to be what I saw then as success in my state. You've heard of the real McCoy, well I thought this may just be him, but he would turn out to be a demon filled McCoy in every sense of the word.

Mind you, I'm writing a book of overcoming, winning, and stories are being submitted, so the clever and crafty move of the enemy was to come to me with a story to share. I was open and because I wasn't staying in my WORD as instructed, but thought because I knew it, I was safe, I was okay. I was praying. I was quoting scripture. But I was not studying as before nor fellowshipping with others as maybe I should. I was taking on a major world/international mission without a covering or a person or persons touching and agreeing with me, to cover me and keep me lifted. I had one dear friend sending me scripture in sermons, but I didn't make the time to stop and take in that she'd sent and trust and believe, God was using her, because after this cross over I listened to nearly every one of them and thought, oh my, if only I'd slowed down to take the time to listen. Everything she'd sent to me was pertaining to where I was walking into. I believe it would have turned the events in my life drastically, but for whatever reason I had to go through it to testify over coming out of it all with Jesus. I now make the time to stop, look, and listen. I would not see what was before me, nor hear, and ended up opening up sharing too much of me with the wrong person.

Though there were red flags, I thought the God in me was going to help me help him see, I'm not a threat but here to help. But if no one has asked for help they evidently don't feel they need it. Lesson learned to live well enough alone.

Interjection: (A respected friend had connected us and in my research of him I saw he was connected to some pastor connections who were replying on his post, so he must be ok right? NO, instead of seeking God's approval, praying, I took the connection from this friend and what I thought I was looking at on FB posts as approval.)

Though I had a check in my spirit of danger, my mind said the situation is not that bad, and I thought I was in control. Being in a mentally drained, medicated, and depressed state only intensified that which would come. KEY WORD IS (I). I of my own-self can do nothing and I, my own-self, walked through those doors to a person, filled with demons, that meant to kill me mind, body, and soul, LITERALLY!

John 10:10-29 (ESV)
[10] *The thief comes only to steal and kill and destroy. I came that they may have life and have it abundantly.* [11] *I am the good shepherd. The good shepherd lays down his life for the sheep.*

I had always been the most conservative of girl. We sat we talked, and his forward nature was an attraction, but I was not prepared for what would come next. I was/am on medication and my motor and thinking skills are not as quick, but I've been able to function without problems. I also was in safe places where harm wouldn't and hadn't ever come. I'd taken all medication this day as well, because I didn't want to appear as limited, as I can be when in pain and trying to impress and not appear so handicapped, outside of my walker, I made sure my appearance of pain was limited. This allowed my lack of response to the actions to come. I shouldn't have even been out, but home sleep when medicated. I'd learned to press through to do what needed to be done feeling I'm controlling myself in the press. So wrong on so many levels because disobedience in the small things carry on over into the major things, and things that matter most are often compromised. I'd been confined, spending much time alone, overwhelming issues with my children, family, ex-husband, church folks, having all my items purposely thrown away, and my own inner turmoil from my accident, so having someone who'd take the time to listen and see pass all of this was a draw and I found rest and found comfort in the wrong place.

Well needless to say, I was there with this full-on aggression in this person and things happened very quickly. I said no or what are you doing we can't/shouldn't, but every touch broke the push away. He was like you know this is what you want. (Be Mindful Who You Let Put Their Hands on You), a touch is powerful. Being alone and by myself for so long the flesh gave way. Everything was going in slow motion. I looked at him but couldn't speak. I had no pleasure from this at all. Honestly, I tried to get into it, but there was nothing, I was in motion and numb to it all. Truth is if you've had the touch of a companion, you desire it unless God has stripped it away and that's not me.

I wanted out but couldn't move, I was stuck. He was only touching me with his hand and that couldn't be so bad, right? I thought to my self.

During and after, I was like oh my goodness, how did I get here. Things happened so fast, though it was playing out in slow motion in my head. I didn't want this to happen. I went to just talk and get to see where the photo shoot would take place and the video for my speaking engagements would be. That's what he told me. He was insisting I come before to see his set up. I refused several times and then a coupled days before I was to meet him, I said ok, I'll come today. The atmosphere was overwhelming and gripping. Trying to wrap my mind around it and wanting to run and hide, disappear somewhere were my thoughts. He came at me and grabbed my breast and it was over. To be honest with you I still don't know what happened and I'm yet puzzled by the spiritual hold that was in that home and over me.

NOT ME, THE CHURCH GIRL, THE PASTOR! I'm writing about winning and now this. Not realizing the fact of the matter was to bring my testimony of winning to a halt with shame and to close my mouth so I would not and could not proclaim Jesus name, BUT

GOD. Winning, yeah right now tell your winning story, AGAIN BUT GOD. I won't lie, it took me a moment to shake what had just happened. The thoughts of how I can speak on winning when it seems I just lost in my testimony of loving Jesus. I'd just went against that I direct people out of, in and with the WORD.

We sat, we talked and then he shared even more about himself and the veil began to unravel. We talked about the certificates on his wall. I guess I'd asked a question. He went on to say that only one of them was real. I was in shock. He does FB lives all the time with the certificates in the background, but they are all fake for the exception of one.
(Interesting to see, that the background scene has since changed, because he shared with me concerning those certificates. Even the enemy is served notice and wise.)

Then we ended up on the subject about his brother. He was leaving his local lawn business with his brother, as he was preparing to move to Atlanta. That move we had previously talked about how we could work together in business covering 2 cities and beyond with the team. Well, he went on to say how his brother went to jail for 20 years, recently was released, and his brother didn't commit the crime. He knew and others knew it to be a fact. He knew the brother wasn't their because he was the one there with others. I realized he quickly closed his mouth because again he'd finally shared too much with me, but it was too late. At this point every blinded shield I had put on was opened, and I was like what in the ham and cheese have I gotten myself into for real. This person has no soul, no heart, NO CONVICTION. Still trying to process what I'm hearing, I'm praying, Lord get me out is the only thing I could think. I realize this guy is a predator and probably a serial predator because he uses fake stuff to lure people in. I'm sure I'm not the only one. My mind is going, but I'm still stuck here.

Now telling this story was never my intent. Honestly, I don't know the fullness of why I must now, but obedience. I've been beat enough from not being obedient and I don't want any more lashes. I wanted to bury this experience right there and leave it, but what greatest freedom is to be transparent before those you have been called to win for the KINGDOM. My experience will be the break for another telling their story for freedom. Ministers lay their life on the line and our transparency shows others how God's Love can and will bring them out of any situation when presented from the heart. I cried out and sought help because I needed this attachment of sin off me. I didn't want anything in me that would hurt my Father. I pleaded with God to cut it from my soul and purify me to not let flesh ever rise again. In the shower scrubbing and scrubbing, with tears, to get it off but it would take an inner cleansing of my soul to free me which would come, thus able to direct others out of the warfare of our lives.

Well after his hand touching he says I just want to touch it one time and he put on protection. I was still looking like what in the world is happening to me. Well he did put protection on, but I feel he'd punctured it with a hole or something. Why do you say this? Because I remember looking down at the package before he put it on and he quickly placed his hand over it and moved it away so I couldn't see while he was touching me with his hand. I remembered seeing and because I was still in slow process mentally and I hadn't done this in sooooo long, it wasn't connecting. He also let me see it on him at the end, but I remember there being something odd in my spirit. Again, I was seeing but not seeing because everything was very slow mentally to me. This scene has played over and over in my brain as well(at least what I remember), and I found it quite strange. He asked me several times later if I was okay. He'd planned to do wrong by me, but I was still clueless to so much trying to figure out how I'd land here in the first place. Thank God whatever he tried to do didn't work, it failed.
My body was in extra pain, so medicating to bring calm back to my body from the added activity (movement in activity) was where I

was at this point and never going back into that was forefront on my mind. Crazy, my doctor had asked if I'd engaged in sexual activity to see what my limitations were since my accident. Not expecting to tell him, but now, I could actually say, physically it's a killer to do what is normal in a relationship with a husband.

This is why as believers we are never to go alone, but sometimes we think we're grown. Not grown in age sense but spiritual sense. I had not stuck to protocol.

I also remember he was conversating with someone before and after. He and someone had planned for this attack. They were working together. He knew more of me than I of him and they'd planned this encounter. I can say this with assurance because God told me. This was planned and I saw it all in a dream and remembered things that were happening as I was coming back to myself. I wasn't fully present thus it took reaching out for help, asking God to reveal to me, me, seeking his face, and being told to cut back the medications with more natural herbs and ingredients. I have continued to hear an audible voice tell me what I need to get and eat and as I look this stuff up after awakening. It's amazing that it all has to do with inflammation and healing. I'm yet using my medication but in intervals with that I hear to use naturally.

The DECEPTION Had Taken Place and I realized, and I questioned it, the deceiver is real and not to be taken lightly. Warfare is real and we need to be taught how to battle because though I'd been through attacks, there was nothing like this I'd been through. Not that I didn't know this, but I realize this was a situation more for me than anything. God was awakening me to hidden things inside and stripping away to truly purify my soul completely, moving me closer to HIS plan and purpose in strength. I needed to learn what it means to battle and arise out of what appears to be the greatest storm of my life.

I had taken matters into my own hands and allowed myself to go against that I believed, because I wanted to think I just may be his change agent in the lives of others. (Change agent). Where in the world was all this coming from? I'd opened to this speaker/ trainer world at a greater level. I was trying to create ways to make money after being down for over 3 years without working due to my accident. Being able to obtain certifications and the like from, "My Healing Bed" must be of God. I'm going to find a way and press in. In my mind and by the words of my mouth, my focus was Kingdom, but my actions proved I had no trust in my God, thus the focus had truly become world. I was trying to make things happen instead of sitting back relying on HIM, GOD, to make a way and supply all my needs according to HIS Riches. I was looking with the natural eye of not working and being able to take care of myself and not trusting that God would truly supply ALL my needs, as HE'd done up to this point and would always. The attacks were great, and I was determined to prove what I, again there is that (I), could do even though things seemed physically stacked against me. My flesh was overriding my spirit and it should have been the other way around.

Though I have good days, I still must lay in bed for days to recuperate from the good day's activities. It's not easy not being about to actively do all I could do before being hit as a pedestrian, an accident I walked away from, going to a cane, and then a wheelchair, now on a walker, and pain increasingly got worse verses better with therapy.

HOW DID THIS HAPPEN?

Remember what I've been doing in this season. I've been on a mission to transform lives for the good through writing this collaborative book on winning. He came with a story. What he had shared previously with me were very personal things, but didn't' include such deception and evil plotting, of course, in our talks. This man's brother spent 20 years locked away for him, WOW, and he let him. And though he was truly taking care of his brother now, that's some twisted mess.

No amount of buying a person a brand-new vehicle or any material gain can measure up to or make up for 20 years of a person's life taken away, locked away, to save your own skin. Moreover, the way I entered the room we were in, I didn't and couldn't notice what was around in the room. I literally was not all together in mind, giddy, naïve, and trusting but when I went out of the room, I saw a camera. I asked if it was on and he said no, but my gut said this was a trap and plan from the start. It was like a sucker punch feeling in my gut, but I moved on and left. (But if you happen to see me out there, prayerfully not, let me know so that I can report it and get justice. It was not with consent for sure. I'm not afraid to fight for my rights.
If he lied the truth will eventually come to light.)
The only time he had consent to film and picture me was for new photo opts for my speaking and consultant branding. He'd shared where he'd helped others turn their brand around and how he could help me. He'd helped them with their Facebook pages and websites, so yes, I though I could allow him to help me. He sent me really nice pics at first and then upon accepting the product the pictures seemed to turn almost demon possessed.
I remember him asking about my story I'd shared about being assaulted in college and what that looked like. All this is told in my Taught to Pray, Left as Prey book. He kept wanting me to video the part where I'd gone to the doctor and my ignorance in that matter when in school, but I told him, not yet it's told in my book. I wanted the book to be the first introduction to what I'd experienced in my college years. He became irritated but I didn't care. Not realizing he himself was about to assault me and that's why he was so persistent.
My story would be released in my time. The videoing was uncomfortable because it brought out raw emotions of how I felt about my situation, especially when I talked about the affect it had on my children and our family connection, but he was encouraging saying, people will relate to the emotions, that's what will sell, and they'll connect for services. The need to succeed in this place of my life was clouding my vision and I was trusting man where I was

supposed to be trusting God, which I honestly thought I was trusting and felt HE'd sent me help.

Get my book Taught to Pray, Left As Prey and you'll understand more about what he wanted to capture on film but this shoot was about my accident and new birth in life so I didn't' go there. I was drugged and assaulted in that book. He was crafty and up to something more deceitful then, but I was just trying to get what I paid for and get out. I should have just left the money on the table and not shown up, but I didn't.

I'm reminded of my old pastor telling a story about how monkeys are caught in the wild in Africa. They put a jar of peanuts out and the monkey comes, puts its hand in the jar, grabs a hand full of nuts, but can't pull his hand out because his hand is in a fist form filled with nuts. Well the capture or killer of the monkey comes, and all the monkey has to do is drop the nuts in its hand and run off but it can't let go of the nuts, or refuses to let go of the nuts and the head is chopped off.

Crazy scenario but true. Oftentimes it's best to just cut your losses in some cases. I felt I'd lost enough and was yet holding on to the little I had to get more verses seeing ALL I NEEDED, I, ALREADY, had in JESUS. My Trust in my Father was dim, but through this HE was teaching me a lesson in TRUST and what that truly is. Without the foundation in HIM from my youth, I probably wouldn't have been able to tell this story or be here completing this book. I also realize HE is always with us, because HE was talking, I was just paralyzed physically and mentally, unable to respond out loud.

I take full responsibility for my actions, because I knew better, BUT I DIDN'T
DO BETTER. I'D PLACED MYSELF IN THIS SITUATION though mentally and spiritually tired, I should have done better. The medication wasn't helping but making me withdraw and see things

differently as well. Mentally, the meds caused me the inability to focus even more, though I still thought I was in control. We become weak to the enemy when we don't stay in our places of prayer and reading the WORD. When we don't face self. I simply was DISOBEDIENT, feeling down, depressed, but not wanting to admit that because it went against what I'd been taught in church. Because this guy had been keeping conversation with me almost daily, he was a call away to just connect. BE CAREFUL WITH WHOM YOU ALLOW CONVERSTATIONS, BECAUSE THOSE PEOPLE BECOME CONECTING POINTS.

TRANSPARENCY

One might say why share such a story. Take it to the Lord in prayer and live it there. Yep, most times this is exactly what I'd do. Truly, this is what I wanted to do. That is what is most important, but too often we leave these devils uncovered to continue hurting others or hurting ourselves. I don't want anyone to feel the pain afflicted in my spirit, mind, and body. I say YES TO SPEAKNG UP, the devil would want to torment me in silence and keep me bound and it's not going to happen as it has happened to too many others and continues. I'm free! I went in there and came out the same person with the same calling, but I realized I had to make some major adjustments. Fasting, praying, and surrounding myself with WORD and WORD folks, people who would and could pray for me, with me, and most of all praying for myself. Sitting my tail down to be fed for a moment was the prescription for the season and that's exactly what I'm doing. Having a local covering is also key. Aside from this mission and some specific things already in hand, I won't take up another thing until released.

Psalm 1 (KJV)

1 Blessed is the man that walketh not in the counsel of the ungodly, nor standeth in the way of sinners, nor sitteth in the seat of the scornful.² But his delight is in the law of the LORD; and in his law doth he meditate day and night.³ And he shall be like a tree planted by the rivers of water, that bringeth forth his fruit in his season; his leaf also shall not wither; and whatsoever he doeth shall prosper. ⁴ The ungodly are not so: but are like the chaff which the wind driveth away.⁵ Therefore the ungodly shall not stand in the judgment, nor sinners in the congregation of the righteous.⁶ For the LORD knoweth the way of the righteous: but the way of the ungodly shall perish.

I'D NEVER BEEN IN THIS KIND OF A SITUATION as an adult or a child. As written in my book Taught to Pray, Left as Prey, I was with a person I truly knew but I was drugged. Funny thing how this all happened. I'd shared the story with him, and he was hell bent on me telling a particular part of my story from that book in a video. I told him it wasn't time, but when I tell you he was fixated on that one piece of my story. I pray and I trust God at an even greater level today when it comes to connecting with anyone.

MY QUESTIONS

What was different this time? How did I lose control? Where Had I allowed my discernment to disconnect from the spirit? I never hurt anyone and always strived to help everyone, why me? What is lacking in me that caused me to even entertain this kind of a guy. Why with him? Truly felt like a mental retardation moment, and that's no disrespect to those who suffer with this, but IS THERE SUCH THING AS SPIRITUAL RETARDATION? I'd been able to keep myself, but truth be told, the conversations with others, who weren't on the same playing field began to open my spirit up to looking flesh-ward rather than Godward.
I'd laugh things off instead of cutting them off. Where was my trust in my God? I realized this person knew who I was, and my beliefs

and he sought to bring harm. Well, the act alone is natural and I'm single.
BUT IN MY CALLING, I WAS OH SO WRONG. The REAL shame, pain, and forgiveness I faced was that of not standing firm in my upbringing and dishonoring ABBA. You see my faith and belief in God had not changed, but going against the proper representation of HIS name, now that is what brought my greatest pain. I cried and cried out with a repentant heart. Where I thought I'd felt brokenness, this experience truly brought on a new level of breaking. A breaking I never in life never, ever, want to experience again. GOD chastises those HE loves, and this was a breaking to build an even greater Kingdom warrior in me. I rise as HE, because greater is He in me. There still was purifying needing to take place, I realized.

CONVICTION

It is that pain and hurt we feel when we are truly sorry about something we've done, that we wouldn't normally do.
We oftentimes overlook this pain and what it is and go into depression, self-condemnation, world condemnation, and allowing people to run us from that God has placed in us verses seeing the gift of conviction being the true display of our heart for God. No sugar coating it, but I had a real human moment that ripped my heart to pieces because of my Love for the Father. In this, I'm being taught what I didn't know about HIS LOVE and being drawn closer and groomed to stand taller and wiser to withstand the things to come. I know not of, but know things are coming down that we must be truly rooted and grounded IN THE WORD to withstand. (Wow, that's another story and this is only small bits to another book that will be written If He Delays His Coming.)
I realized after I collected myself that I had encountered the devil himself in human form. No, really, that's what I heard in spirit. BUT WHAT HE DIDN'T REALIZE WAS THAT I WAS GOING TO SOUND THE ALARM EVEN GREATER FOR THE LORD. I AM GOING TO BE ON THE MOUNTAIN TOP SHOUTING

FROM THE ROOF TOP, JESUS IS LORD. Yes, I messed up royally, not understanding the royalty that I belong. The devil will not steal the joy I have on this mission of being an overcomer and sharing stories of the same. He Tried, But It Didn't Work! Yes, flesh makes me think on things at times, but the WORD of God washes it away.

My actions in this place may have displaced the average person, but average I'm not and I know this because God has told me. I'm still learning even more about that HE has given me, for my greatest work in HIM for HIS Kingdom to come.
I'm reminded of the journey of David, in the BIBLE. A man after God's own heart who fell many times but ended up writing those beautiful, heart wrenching prayers, (in Psalms), crying out and asking for forgiveness, strength, and guidance. He was the apple of God's Eye. Not because he did no wrong, but because He WAS A MAN AFTER GOD's OWN HEART WITH REAL CONVICTION. Now truth be told there are things he lost because of his acts but he didn't' lose his position God had given him. My faith in why Jesus came trumps those losses, and gains us Kingdom eternal living as the conviction, knowledge, and wisdom of HIM make us have a heart to repent, be strengthened, renewed, restored, and changed to continue.
Staying connected to the WORD Helps us remember the reason for HIS coming, HIS death, burial, and resurrection of victory. It shows us how to win battles and how to fight wars. I'm a little different and it's okay. I love working in the field and helping people, but in this season, I must be a little selfish and help myself. I must allow my soul to be fed and built up. Sometimes we can give and give and never take the time to receive leaving place for error.

I HAD TO ASK ABBA TO SHOW ME, ME, to worship HIM in Spirit and in Truth. Amazingly, though I've worn my smile and continued to show love, I was deeply hurting inside. DEPRESSION was there, but never experiencing it or having a reference, I'd been in a state of Functional Depression. Yes, a new WORD with great

meaning. I'd been able to function outwardly on the outside and even mentally in a functioning capacity, though broken and hurting and in pain. My previous church affiliation had taking its toll and pushed me over the edge, combined with others previous religious affiliations, and I'd become isolated and functioning alone. Not the accident, but the pain of being left alone due to doctrinal beliefs and the ostracizing of a group of people I'd opened my heart to and believed in as family, but far from the truth. Learning that the associate pastor was a private investigator and being told things had been placed in my home when they came to clean it. The person who appeared and came around as a sister only to complete a task disappearing, a pastor who said we're coming to see you on Wednesday and
Wednesday never came and no calls were returned, no emails answers as to where they were or if they were coming another day, yes and sooooo much more. All because I was an ordained minister in the WORD, and they didn't believe in women ministers and they believe in shutting you down if you don't comply with what they believe. Yes, I don't bite my tongue on any of it. As I come into the knowledge of the belief's I even went to the head pastor whom I love dearly and his wife, who have both left that church. I wanted them to know who I was, but that I yield under them when in that ministry. I wanted them to know up front that I do other things in the community. They prayed with me and I thought it was over. It wasn't in the eyes of some, but only the beginning of hell on earth in the 4 walls of religion. This along with being physically incapacitated, after being hit by a vehicle as a pedestrian, all combined crushed me. Dealing with things even from my youth and family issues in the now all added to what could have been my death spiritually and physically. The isolation left me more vulnerable than I'd imagined until this incident with this guy, placing my life in the hands of evil blindly, and the crying out because of what I did in disbelief of finding myself in this kind of state that awoke me to shake me, slap me back into reality of THIS IS NOT YOU. REMEMBER MY CHILD YOUR HERITAGE AND CALL.

HEAR YOUR FATHER.
The isolation was the weapon formed, BUT GLORY BE TO GOD IT DID NOT PROSPER. I DIDN'T DIE IN THIS STATE BUT AROSE WITH POWER TO TELL THE STORY IN A GREATER PLACE YET WINNING NO MATTER WHAT.

I did and reached out to my soon to be pastor and told him I needed prayer, I'd fallen hard, but I'm not afraid and transparency. I had strength to open my mouth and ask and seek HELP. Pride had no place and has no place when you are yielded for HIS Glory to be used beyond yourself for souls. I knew at this point I was going to be alright and the enemies hold to silence me and keep be isolated was broken, as I reached out to an elder as the WORD instructs us. I trusted, this pastor to say HELP me in prayer. The fact that I could break free and open my mouth gave God All POWER again, as I released the control, I had in suffering alone. The yoke meant to bind me was instantly broken when I opened my mouth.

I continue the journey the devil sought to snatch away. I'M NOT GIVING UP ANOTHER THING GOD HAS GIVEN ME AND THAT IS WITHOUT DOUBT. You see we are giving things up often, and due to the lack of Truth, it's causing us to turn, run, and/or forfeit what we have rights to. God tells us that what HE gives us can't be taken from us, yet we do have the choice in giving it up. I (God) am with you ALWAYS, is the WORD. NOT ME, with God's Help, I'm taking it all back and not releasing another thing!
In this case not only had I stumped my toe, I skinned my knees, elbows, face, and knocked out teeth in the spirit realm. Spiritually, I was like a boxer who got in the ring talking much trash and came out bloodied, swollen, and blue, on a stretcher, because I forgot what my trainer had taught me, had fail to remember// keep the manual (BEING THE BIBLE) before me, and was in my flesh verses connected to and in the Spirit as I thought I was. Not to make light of it, but this thing was real. These things are real. This thing hit

hard. I took blows. I'm yet being mended, tended to, and healing in my spirit and life.

Romans 11:29
For the gifts and calling of God are without repentance.

It's hard enough that you've failed God, but to know your radar was so off or was it. Hearing about someone's molestation, parentless life, never being loved, nor in love, made me feel I had power to help because of the God LOVE in me. I'd love you and show you it's possible to love and be loved. The blows were strong in the home front and I guess I wanted to feel love too. NOT MY PLACE at least not in this space of no union or unity. God was all the LOVE I needed and will ever need. The trickery and scheme of the devil who knows us at times more than we know our selves is what we must be aware of. He sits back and plots in quiet, while keeping us busy in good to do things, not God directed things, so that we are off focus and not taking proper time to connect with God.

The transforming and renewing of one's mind can only come from the Spirit of God and the Holy Ghost. Though we know this, being in ministry you are afforded the opportunity to see miracles and those life changes before your eyes, and if not careful, you can get beside yourself and try to operate outside of the anointing on your own, thinking you're In the Spirit and it's all flesh.

The only thing that can be destroyed on this earth is my body and I yield that to the Lord. I will live and not die to declare the works of the lord. My mind, soul, and spirit belong to the LORD and will return to HIM. I stand believing that Jesus is Lord and that HE was and is God in Flesh who came to be crucified, dying for my sins, and rise to show HE had the power and victory in HIS hands with the keys to break the yoke and chains off my neck to live free. My conviction to cry when I don't look like ABBA is a gift. This is a gift to us all. Without the truth of knowing this is a gift, you can easily move into condemnation and worldly conviction that kills us from within and bleeds out. This kind of attack slows our walk and makes us feel we didn't' really know HIM and we don't deserve HIM. Thinking and being taught we must start all over again when we fall, which is not the case. In actuality, HIS call is even greater upon us when the enemy comes in like a flood and HE Lifts Up A Standard. Problem is we get drowned in the flood part and forget, there is a Lifting connected if we faint not and remember what A FATHER's LOVE looks like, feels like, and what it is all about.

The conviction I've experienced, let's me know that I am still HIS own.

No one truly wants to disappoint a parent, except a person who never knew the love of their parent which makes it easy to be used to destroy and try and destroy others. I pray God's mercy for them and the ones who have been used to try to assassinate me. He is and they are broken as we all have been, but some of us have been captured by the LOVE of JESUS and others haven't and have stiffed necks and hardened hearts. Hurting people truly hurt people. GOD is the parent of all parents and the one you want to be proud when you are before HIM, in HIS Presence.

I thought I knew brokenness, but this here, broke me down, because of MY DADDY, ABBA. HIS Kingdom takes enough hits and I surely didn't want to be another cause of hits from within HIS camp. I don't want to give the world another reason to say HE isn't real, and the church folks are fake and hypocritical. I'm here to say don't judge God by me, I

AM A SINNER BOUGHT BY GRACE AS WE ALL ARE, and where I fail as a human, GOD NEVER FAILS (Keep Your Eyes on HIM).

The wages of sin is death and JESUS paid the price and collected it all back, by defeating death for our victory.

You see, as a child learns from the correction of a parent, so is the conviction in our hearts to want to grow up looking like and mimicking those who've loved us and nurtured us, mainly our parents. I realize though no parent wants a child to fail or fall, those are that child's experiences to make them better human beings if they are learning from those experiences. These are their own personal testimonies God will use to bring healing. Also, when that child falls, the parent doesn't say you are not mine. No, they help the child up and tell them to try it again. God tells us to get up, I've Got You!

Thinking of the prodigal son and his brother. The eldest brother stayed home and did everything he was told but the prodigal son in the BIBLE, the youngest took his inheritance and lived a wildlife. After losing all he had, he remembered that his father had much wealth and even eating in the fields as a servant was better than where he'd found himself or that he'd walked into. He took responsibility and at this point he'd return, and his father would not just welcome him back home, but he'd have the fatted calf prepared in celebration.

THIS IS THAT WHICH TAKES PLACE IN THE SPIRIT WHEN WE STOP MAKING EXCUSES, TRULY YIELD, REPENT, AND BE CONVERTED, REALIZING WE ARE ONE WITH HIM NOT SEEING HIM OUTSIDE OF US. ABBA'S ARMS ARE OUTSTRETCHED, AND HE MEETS US AND GREETS US RIGHT WHERE WE ARE AT. HE MADE US AND KNOWS US AND WE ARE FROM HIM IF WE RECOGNIZE AND RECEIVE TRUTH.

Navigating points through life to eventually and ultimately arrive when life's all over at the destination of eternal forever is this I'm speaking of. The beauty in that is, it begins right here on earth. Just as being married, doesn't begin when you marry, the seed and preparation in heart begins long before that person comes along. The heart is already conditioned and prepared. The older are to teach the younger to be winners in their marriages.

Yes, there is freedom that comes in sharing my story. Truth is life happenings doesn't negate my call or belief nor yours. Conviction and true repentance to be better, do better, and grow closer not continuing in the same mess/path, but graduating day by day, year by year, to look more and more like HIM, is the process in gaining spiritual muscles in which to stand firm and accounted for in the end.
We must become One with HIM.
It's all about, LOVE, ACTION, DEED, and LIFE LIVING. I'm taking responsibility for my actions, not making excuses, changing to worship HIM in Spirit and in Truth is my driving force.

We are overcome by the words of our testimony and though this, my testimony, isn't pretty and refined, it's my story. It isn't as I'd hoped, that when I gave my life I'd never fall or sin, not like this, but when we are broken and not understanding how to deal with it, we leave ourselves prey. It is my hope and prayer that where you are torn down, you are built up. Where you are weak, you are made strong. Where you are blind, your eyes are opened so you can see. AND THOUGH I've fallen and will fail, I pray that you Will ALWAYS See the Love of Jesus In Me.

I've yielded myself completely to the FATHER in a way I've never known before, thinking I'd already done so. HE knew what it would take to awaken me to complete TRUTH and understanding and though not HIS will, this occurrence has drawn me closer and into a greater relationship with HIM. What was meant to bring me darkness brought me to the greater LIGHT. So, I share with you a prayer:

(KJV) Psalm 51: 1 Have mercy upon me, O God, according to thy lovingkindness: according unto the multitude of thy tender mercies blot out my transgressions. 2 Wash me throughly from mine iniquity, and cleanse me from my sin. 3 For I acknowledge my transgressions: and my sin is ever before me. 4 Against thee, thee

only, have I sinned, and done this evil in thy sight: that thou mightest be justified when thou speakest, and be clear when thou judgest. *5 Behold, I was shapen in iniquity; and in sin did my mother conceive [1] me. 6 Behold, thou desirest truth in the inward parts: and in the hidden part thou shalt make me to know wisdom.*

7 Purge me with hyssop, and I shall be clean: wash me, and I shall be whiter than snow. 8 Make me to hear joy and gladness; that the bones which thou hast broken may rejoice. 9 Hide thy face from my sins, and blot out all mine iniquities. 10 Create in me a clean heart, O God; and renew a right [2] spirit within me. 11 Cast me not away from thy presence; and take not thy holy spirit from me. 12 Restore unto me the joy of thy salvation; and uphold me with thy free spirit. 13 Then will I teach transgressors thy ways; and sinners shall be converted unto thee.

What Will Keep Us: **THE CLEANSING BLOOD OF JESUS & STAY**ING **IN THE WORD**, LITERALLY!

THE STRUGGLE IS REAL BUT SO IS MY GREAT GOD, YAHWEH, JEHOVAH!
WHAT THE DEVIL MEANT FOR BAD, GOD TURNED

IT FOR MY GOOD!!!!

Bottom line is I had to see me and not all the hurts and pains. Truth is people hurt us and we hurt people because of life experiences and spiritual attacks. It's not until we face ourselves, change really come. It wasn't about anybody else but the term oil going on within, the enemy within me, that I had to face to gain real independence and freedom for Impact in the Kingdom

All About Souls Souls Souls
Beginning With My Own Soul
By: Shermanda Ramsay

Hebrews 12:6-11 (NLT)

⁶ For the LORD disciplines those he loves,   and he punishes each one he accepts as his child."[a]

⁷ As you endure this divine discipline, remember that God is treating you as his own children. Who ever heard of a child who is never disciplined by its father? ⁸ If God doesn't discipline you as he does all of his children, it means that you are illegitimate and are not really his children at all. ⁹ Since we respected our earthly fathers who disciplined us, shouldn't we submit even more to the discipline of the Father of our spirits, and live forever?[b]

¹⁰ For our earthly fathers disciplined us for a few years, doing the best they knew how. But God's discipline is always good for us, so that we might share in his holiness. ¹¹ No discipline is enjoyable while it is happening—it's painful! But afterward there will be a peaceful harvest of right living for those who are trained in this way.

Looking at the beautiful task and movement in my hands is proof of the change we have been called to bring to this world. True stories of our lives to shed light and bring hope. It helps others see they are not alone. If you and I can overcome the same adversities operating in the earth realm daily, others can surely be strengthened, encouraged, and inspired to do the same. As one of the authors states, "we have to embrace the good, the bad, and the ugly." In doing so, we embrace truth, for transformation, and allowing our minds to be renewed to do better, be better, and live our greatest lives WINNING, In A Winning World.

I'm honored to share this book with these amazing stories of overcomers from around the world. Every story is unique and different. Reaching out to touch the hearts of those who can relate and break the cycle of self-defeat, depression, self-hate and living amazing lives working out our own soul salvation, working out our lives on purpose, to victory!

Where you are broken there is a mending. Where you were lost, you are found. Where you'd given up, you now have hope. Where it was dark, you now see the light. You will take up your bed and walk. You will live in victory. No matter your struggle today, great or small, You are a winner, winning!

Say this with me:
WINNING IS MY BIRTH RIGHT!

I love each of you, no matter where you are, or what you are going through. If you are reading this, you have life and breath in your body and there is a purpose and plan for your life. You are somebody! You are loved! You are prayed for! It is hoped for you to fulfill the greatness you are and have been granted to carry out and WIN from your conception election.

I would love to hear from you! Tell us your story.
(Story Submissions for Book Edition 2020 has begun)

I WANT EVERYONE TO REALIZE WE ALL GO THROUGH AND IF YOU NEED HELP, SAY HELP. YOU CAN'T GET WHAT YOU DON'T ASK FOR. GOD WILL COME IF YOU CALL AND HE WILL SEND YOUR ANSWERS JUST WAIT ON IT!

From Shermanda's Healing Bed She's Obtained the Following:

Personal Website: https://shermanda.com/

JMT Webpage: http://www.johnmaxwellgroup.com/ShermandaRamsay

Founder Trainer/ Coach	Certified- Corporate Business Consultant Trainer	Founding Member Les Brown M.A.T. Speaker, Trainer, Coach

Author and Publisher of Write Road Publishing

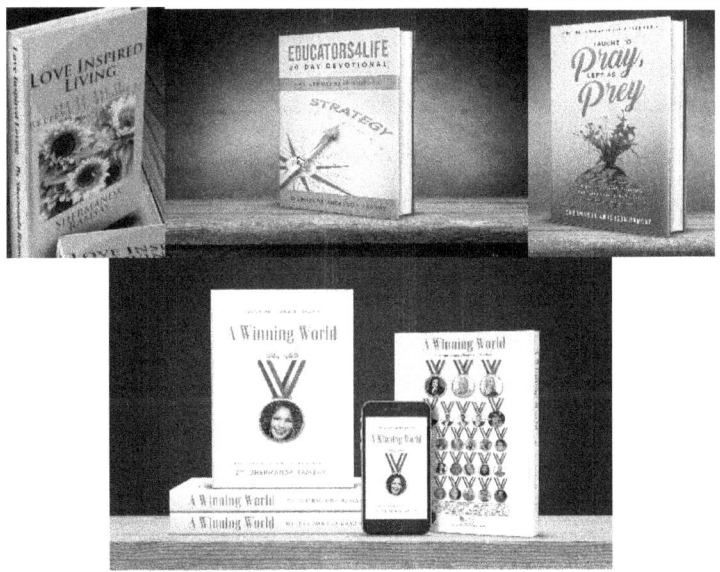

Radio Show on SATURDAY's @ 11am
(91.7fm- Jax; 91.3fm- GA;91.9fm- St. Augustine)

YouTube: (Subscribe to page):
https://www.youtube.com/channel/UCSA9hy80AVpnRZ6p6qYD77A?view_as=subscriber

Websites: https://awinningworld.com/
https://shermanda.com/a-winning-world/
Facebook: https://www.facebook.com/awinningworld/
Twitter: https://twitter.com/awinningworld

Sponsored By:

Revelation 12:11 (KJV)

¹¹ And they overcame him by the blood of the Lamb, and by the word of their testimony; and they loved not their lives unto the death.

REVIEWS

"The truth has made me free as I know it will for you, as you tell your story with undeniable proofs.
You will discover that the pages of this book are invigorating, life changing, and resourceful, which will lead to a victorious lifestyle if you select to view life through your spiritual lens. It is a detailed journey of experiences leading to optimal health in mind, body, and soul. Enjoy the journey as we all should speak to be understood,"
~ L. Sanders

"Shermanda is a beautiful speckle of hope and inspiration plowing through her physical challenges while sharing her gift with the world. Her loyalty and faith know no bounds. Her <u>A Winning World</u> project and collaborative work is uplifting, motivational, encouraging and is sure to give you the strength and perseverance to never give up!" Because of Shermanda, I feel stronger and more capable than ever in my ability to serve the world,"
~ A. Dickson

These stories have greatly inspired me, and they have also given me strength and taken away my doubts. I'm now more focused on what I can do verses what I can't do. I truly believe that I can do what I put my mind to with Christ as my guide. I'm so motivated, I've decided to go back to school after reading these amazing stories.
~Nascimento

www.ingramcontent.com/pod-product-compliance
Lightning Source LLC
Chambersburg PA
CBHW072134160426
43197CB00012B/2096